WE'VE GOT TO STOP OUR WARS — OR ELSE!

WE'VE GOT TO STOP OUR WARS — OR ELSE!

for all the lively women — or men? on "The View"

Jackie Taylor

JACQUELINE TAYLOR

To order additional copies of this book, contact:
Xlibris Corporation
1-888-795-4274
www.Xlibris.com
Orders@Xlibris.com
44528

CONTENTS

PART 1: PROTESTS AND POEMS

PART 2: SATIRES

PART 3: DRAMA

PART 1

PROTESTS AND POEMS

WE NEED A LAW AGAINST GOING TO WAR—RESPECTING OUR CONSTITUTION

Dwight Eisenhower, the most popular general of World War II and two-term Republican president, said: "In the councils of government we must guard against the acquisition of unwarranted influence, whether sought or unsought, by the military-industrial-complex. The potential for the disastrous rise of misplaced power exists and will persist.

"Every gun that's made, every warship launched, every rocket fired signifies, in the final sense, a theft from those who hunger and are not fed, those who are cold and are not clothed. The world in arms is not spending alone. It is spending the sweat of laborers, the genius of its scientists, the hopes of its children . . . this is not a way of life, in any true sense. Under the cloud of threatening war, it is humanity hanging from an iron cross!"

Strong words . . . have they been forgotten?

Under our guidance, Iraq, suffering and dying under our latest war, formed a Constitution. Our leaders had spoken eloquently of the need for a document like ours for Iraq. But our own Constitution, on the other hand, has been ignored by most of our presidents since the end of World War II. The Constitution states irrevocably that the power and right of declaring war belongs to Congress, only Congress. Thus our Constitution has been violated by Harry Truman, Lyndon Johnson, Ronald Reagan, George H. W. Bush, and George W. Bush.

Our founding fathers worried about the possibility of misused power by future presidents in waging war. So, in spite of our Constitution's clear instruction, there is an obvious need to establish a new law stating that no president may take us to war without the declaration of war by Congress.

Considering how many unnecessary wars our leaders have thrust us into—eight since WWII, Congress should create a law making war possible only if our nation is invaded by a power wanting to take us over—not very likely. The Constitution decrees that Congress maintain the military to "Suppress an Insurrection and Repel an Invasion," no suggestion of traveling far to attack nations that have not harmed us in any way.

Such a law prohibits Japan from going to war. Most of the European nations, having experienced war on their own soil, have given up war and founded a European Union to settle problems diplomatically and peaceably, as urged by President Roosevelt and Britain's Winston Churchill after World War II. Only our own nation still engages in the barbaric cruelty of war, over and over, needlessly, with human losses in the millions.

Thus we must urge our senators and Representatives to begin action for such a law. This would not only save our own and foreign lives, but lower fear, hatred, and desire for terrorism against us.

General-President Eisenhower would approve such a law.

Most of the world's religions, in different words, say "Thou Shalt Not Kill!"

A NEW DANGER IN OUR WAR MAKING—REVENGE

For 57 years, we've enjoyed our many wars, like the Iraq War all unnecessary wars against smaller, weaker countries that had done us no harm, and of course could not resist us. They tried, gallantly, patriotically for their own countries—North Korea, Vietnam, Grenada, Nicaragua, Panama, Iraq, Afghanistan, Iraq again. But the raw power of the United States military might, our billions of dollars focused on means of destruction and death, assured our triumphs: eight wars since WWII, called "The Good War" by Studs Terkel.

Until now, we have suffered no consequences. Those nations we attacked for no valid reason took no revenge for the killing of thousands of human beings in their lands, 3,200,000 Vietnamese killed, 58,000 of our own killed in the Vietnam War alone. Eight wars despite the vividly clear warnings of General and Republican President Eisenhower against the power of the Military Industrial Complex, and his own repulsion at war: "I hate war as only a soldier can who has been there, who has seen its brutality, its futility, its stupidity!"

Indisputably, most of our presidents since Ike have not shared his repulsion at the brutality of war. Since the end of Ike's "Good War," our eight—8—wars have been accomplished with flowing rhetoric from each president who decided on war, each with support of our Congress—more or less, never recalling the impassioned words of the beloved general who at the end of WWII, along with British Winston Churchill and our President Roosevelt, urged our nations never to have another war but settle problems diplomatically. A much neglected word, "diplomatically."

However successful we have been in our wars and scattered coups, we may now have to reconsider our war making: It's become too dangerous. For US!

Yes, of course wars are always dangerous—but now something new has been added—fear of terrorism. A very real fear for Americans. The president has issued his mantra for the past five years—"Since 9/11, since 9/11 . . ." Almost anything is allowed because of "9/11." But gradually, little by little, Americans in high and low places, even many Republicans, are beginning to realize that a group of people does indeed hate us, resent us, and wants to harm us. They are radical Muslims in the Middle East, where we are now engaged in a messy war we can't seem to squeeze out of. Nor can Iraq, suffering civil war, insurgents, tragic numbers of deaths, several million having rushed out of their homeland that, because of our invasion, has become a battleground.

Gradually, many in our government, except our president and his Cabinet, are getting the idea long obvious to many critics, American and Muslim alike—the Muslims don't want us strutting around their part of the world. The longer we stay there, building 14 new bases in Iraq and the world's biggest, most exclusive embassy—all the shops and restaurants an American can want and never have to meet one Iraqi!—and parking our military in several hundred places in the Middle East, they will hate and resent us more—and want to harm us. Can there be any doubts as to their intents—"since 9/11?"

Many years ago, Jimmy Carter said that nations see us as the "world's war monger." Only he and Eisenhower held terms of peace—Kennedy might have had he lived through his term, but when Johnson took over the chance for peace ended. Kennedy himself had said, apparently out of Johnson's earshot: "Mankind must eliminate war, or war will eliminate mankind." And he avoided violent contact with Cuba.

Now with attacks by Muslims against us, with their leaders being specific about their charges and grievances against us, isn't it time we took their warnings seriously in order to avoid more 9/11s?

How many American citizens have learned what Osama bin Laden openly gave as his reasons for 9/11? His first was the deaths of a million Iraqi children caused by impure drinking water due to the Bush One and Tony Blair destruction of Iraq's water purification plants, followed by sanctions, sustained by President Clinton, that forbade imports of chlorine to purify their water. A pretty cruel action to those most vulnerable to impure water—the elderly, children and babies. How many of our citizens have heard about this? Why not?

Although both the president and former Secretary Rumsfeld have stated on TV that "We have no evidence of a connection between Saddam and 9/11," the president began a war in Iraq that has killed hundreds of thousands of

Iraqis—Muslims. Is this the way to win friends in the Muslim-Arab world and diminish hatred and terrorism against us?

How many Muslims or men considered to be Muslims have been grabbed up around the world and imprisoned in detainee camps? How many tortured? These situations can fairly be called "terrorizing"—and admittedly done by our military and CIA personnel. The Muslim world's awareness of these cases must have a negative, an infuriating effect.

And totally overlooked by the White House, by our Congress, by our Media, is that our Constitution states plainly that CONGRESS is to be in charge of "Captures on Land and Waters." Why has Congress neglected this duty in the face of such inhuman, torturous treatment of Muslims or assumed Muslims? Why have they not demanded each location of our places of imprisonment and torture—dishonorable Rendition"?

The citizens in all of our past eight wars—haven't most of them been people of slightly darker skin? Do we think that people around the world haven't noticed this? Especially Muslims, many of whom are dissatisfied with their lives of less wealth and luxury than Americans are known to possess? Many of us?

We need only contemplate how we would feel if our nation were surrounded by soldiers and weaponry of powerful Muslims who had killed thousands of our citizens, destroyed much of our great buildings and infrastructure, historic and cultural landmarks, cutting off clean water and electricity, causing such fear and chaos that millions of our own people were forced to leave their homes and flee to Canada, Mexico, Latin American lands that would accept us. What a terrible thing even to contemplate! But a reality for millions of Iraqis. Can any American accept this, as many bishops and ministers cannot?

Are the president and Vice-Pres actually hoping to make some shocking military strike against Iran now because it just might maybe perhaps have some atomic power we allow other Middle East powers to have—but no, THEY can't? The appallingly unfriendly welcome Ahmadinejad received in our country, especially at the usually judiciously sensible Columbia University, was frustrating to those who realized OUR unfriendly acts toward Iran—in 1954 daring to remove their elected Prime Minister Mossadegh and bring in a Shah more deferential to us; then, during the Reagan years, generously offering our then-pal Saddam Hussein lethal material to throw against Iran. Which power is the danger here?

Despite George W Bush's determination to keep his mistaken war going with cheery mien and no words of regret or compassion, for our own safer future we must end our presence there now. We must urge the United Nations to gather a group of Middle Eastern leaders, perhaps with Nelson Mandela and Desmond Tutu, to work with the disparate factions in Iraq to search for solutions for peace. Then we must provide money and help to reconstruct what we so callously destroyed—and finally learn that military might and military profits must end if our people are to be safer—as General-President Eisenhower urged.

"War on Terrorism" is a metaphor, like the "War on Poverty," that meant seeking ways to lower poverty—not by shooting poor people! "War on Terrorism" really means lowering, ending terrorism. By constantly referring to the "War on Terrorism, "Bush and his Republican allies are trying to make Americans believe that we are killing terrorists and lessening "Terrorism." But can we end hostile feelings and actions toward us by destroying a Muslim country, terrifying two million Muslims to leave for other lands, and killing hundreds of thousands of Muslim Iraqis?

This is clearly a new kind of war for us—the people we have harmed, those whose loved ones we have killed, are not going to forget and forgive us. These Muslims have expressed their feelings—and we are stirring them each day to get vengeance. We MUST face the truth about our needless war-making NOW!

WHOSE PRISON TERM?

There he sat on 60 Minutes, a young soldier accused of killing family members in Iraq, the only one of a group of soldiers so accused who agreed to appear and respond to questions. He's 25, looked like an innocent 17, and spoke softly, almost gently about what he had done—after a buddy was killed by an unseen Iraqi, he and his troop looked around for the perpetrator; not seeing anyone, they rushed toward the nearest building, a home way down a hill, not close by, and tossed in a grenade, killing women and children.

The loss of a buddy by an unseen Iraqi seems the basis for the soldiers' rush for revenge, killing of innocents. These young American soldiers are in prison, awaiting trial and prison terms of five to ten or more years for the crime of killing several innocent civilians. George Bush and Dick Cheney killed 100,000 innocent Iraqis by powerful bombs during their invasion and takeover of Iraq, then paved the way for civil war there, hiking the death toll to more than 750,500 Iraqis, more dying every day.

What will be the prison term of George W. Bush and Dick Cheney?

George H. W. Bush, with Britain and other coalition members, killed a few thousand Iraqis in their attack on Saddam's forces barging into Kuwait in 1991. In that operation, Bush One ordered, likely with Tony Blair's assent, the destruction of water purification and sewage plants, and then imposed sanctions that forbade Iraq's import of chlorine and essential plumbing parts to purify their water, thus causing in the next ten years deaths of a million children and babies, and more than a half million elderly, those most vulnerable to impure water.

What are the prison terms of George H. W. Bush and Tony Blair?

Five years after World War II ended, President Truman, with some U.N. forces, invaded North Korea; North and South Korean civilians and armed forces, plus Chinese soldiers killed—1,600,000; U.S. forces killed, 162,708; U.N. soldiers killed, 17,260.

How many years in prison was President Truman given?

As Senator Kerry, when young, told Congress about his experience in the Vietnam War: all soldiers are not honorable and moral; all kinds of young men are in armies around the world, in an occupation that teaches and commands the killing of fellow human beings, almost always innocent. The military provides the means of killing, training recruits emotionally to hate the designated "enemy," so young soldiers can forget that they are invaders, occupiers, the "enemy" themselves.

When the far, unfamiliar country of North Vietnam appeared to be pushing its communism onto South Vietnam in the early 1960's, President Lyndon Johnson, taut in the grip of the Cold War, began sending our soldiers there to stop the takeover, seeming dismissive of France's earlier defeat there. For almost ten years, Johnson and then Richard Nixon sent thousands of young Americans into that underdeveloped land whose people had not in any way harmed us; they armed our soldiers with bombs, guns speared with bayonets, land mines, Napalm to toss onto girls and boys to burn off their skin, pilots with Agent Orange to spread over forests to defoliate them.

Americans lost, more than 58,000; wounded many times over that, and those with PTSD—Post Traumatic Stress Disorder, uncountable, many still coming into veteran counseling centers for relief from distress and their own acts of violence. Vietnamese citizens killed, according to Johnson's Defense Secretary Robert McNamara—3,200,000.

What was the prison term given Lyndon Johnson? What prison term for Nixon?

Ronald Reagan in his almost secret war with small, impoverished Nicaragua in the 1980's after it ousted a cruel dictator, Somoza, called by President Roosevelt "An S.O.B., but OUR S.O.B.!", used mercenaries from nearby countries, such as Honduras, to kill citizens, bomb bridges, clinics and buses, with a total of Nicaraguans killed, 36,000; Americans killed, none. Mercenaries killed, no record.

What was the prison term for Ronald Reagan?

George H. W. Bush suddenly was irked when his former buddy Noriega of Panama refused to do his bidding, so he sent in his troops to kill a few thousand Panamanians and thrash their way into Panama City to—in violation of international law—kidnap Noriega and bring him into OUR country for trial and imprisonment, in Florida, where he was kept until recently. (One can only imagine what would happen if any foreign power did the same thing to us.)

What prison term did Bush 41 receive?

The deaths of innocents, the deaths of soldiers, are always tragic. Our soldiers, almost all still young, immature, unsure of their ideals and convictions, are ordered to do acts that in civilian life would be shocking and provoke trials and imprisonments. The crimes of young soldiers who needlessly kill innocents on their own is depressing. More depressing, and criminal, are the hundreds of thousands of human beings Bush-Cheney-Wolfowitz-Rumsfeld decided to have killed—men, women, children, babies, in a war of choice against a power that had never harmed us. This is called a pre-emptive war, not Constitutional, considered "our most serious moral problem" by Republican candidate for president, Cong. Ron Paul of Texas.

WASTING 50 YEARS
PROTESTING WARS

Surely there were better things to do

For 50 years I've been wasting my time—protesting one war after another.

Somehow I missed the North Korean War, Truman's initial effort to cut down communism just five years after the end of WW II. Sure, Roosevelt and Churchill and General Eisenhower all said then that we should have no more wars, and Republican Ike, later two-term President, spoke vigorously against war and warned of the dangers and power of the Military Industrial Complex. Who listened? Who cared anyway?

I guess I was having babies during the Korean battle, but when Vietnam came close after, I was ready—marching, writing, visiting senators and Congressmen and newspaper editors—and driving my family wild each time I heard about the deaths of both our hapless soldiers and Vietnamese civilians. I just couldn't see the good side, OUR side, Johnson's side of that conflict. Good lord, I even wrote my first anti-war play! And presenting it in Chicago and its suburbs did NOT stop the war.

So I wasted MY time, my husband's state of mind after working all day in Public Relations, and my daughters' patience while they needed help with school work and washing their blue jeans and blouses. Well, I blame the damn TV news that really showed graphic and shocking pictures in those days, more than they do today, they've learned better, for God's sake, why get people all churned up about stuff they can't do anything about anyway?

Of course it wasn't only the TV news—I always like to find someone or some medium to blame—the fault was MINE! ALL MINE! I didn't have the one thing that keeps people sane and able to be lived with, able to

18

smile with their spouses, play cheerfully with their children, joke with their neighbors—PATRIOTISM!

But somehow PATRIOTISM escaped me. I blame my mother mostly, but listen, when we were kids growing up she had only the BIG ONE, WW II, and she never complained even though she had cousins in Germany. But when I was grown up and married, instead of attempting to muffle me, she went right along with me in getting mad at our wars and shaking her head—she had a terrific head-shake while tightening her lips that only added fuel to my fire!

We shared the fury of Vietnam, all the endless years of it without flinching, I upsetting my school girls who have never quite forgiven me for those years of my fervently expressed rage—was it 9 or 10 or 20 years of that little war?

And then came Ronald Reagan, another president who worried about our frenzied fear of communism and began a low key war in little Nicaragua that had just accomplished a revolution to oust the Saddam-like dictator Somoza, losing 40,000 people but doing well in dealing with the less privileged citizens, eliminating polio within a year, all that good stuff. But Reagan kept referring to their leader, Daniel Ortega, as "That dirty little Commie in designer jeans!"

So he paid a lot of job-seeking men from nearby little places like Honduras to shoot and kill Ortega supporters, civilians in buses, etc. We war protesters took it upon ourselves to stop it—HA! Who did we think we were? God or Nancy Reagan? My girls were in college then, spared my fruitless activism. But my husband had to put up with me, asking, how about a movie or a concert? Come ON! Get off it, will ya? But I couldn't!

It took about eight years, but finally it ended, with some neatly chosen Americans arranging their election without even charging Nicaragua for it, avoiding the success of Ortega's party by creating a coalition of all of the other parties including the REAL Communist party, which we paid to join up! Brilliant! Reagan's Contra had killed 36,000 innocent citizens, sure. But once again, I missed seeing the popular appeal of Reagan, and the popular appeal of gunning down communists too, even if they weren't REAL commies! What was the difference? We didn't even know any Nicaraguans—I had never even BEEN there!

Let's not even mention Grenada, Reagan's grand invasion of a sweet little island. Let's go right to George H. W. Bush and his gallant invasion of Panama to take out his old pal Noriega, who was, silly man, refusing to do Bush's bidding, mostly about Nicaragua, but who knows or cares? It's our God given right to invade and kill a few people and remove anyone we don't like from office. Take him to OUR country, Florida, for trial and imprisonment, keep him there for about 15 years, and let him go without any attention from the media. The story is old and forgotten. BorING!

Late in 1991, foolish Saddam thought he could march into oil fields of Kuwait—whoa! Not a chance! Big Brother is watching and wants to use up some of our fine arms and ammunition so we can make more. So Bush One gathered together a fine little coalition to shove Saddam Hussein out of Kuwait—listen, there's OIL in them thar hills! And it's OURS! So Bush did it all right, used depleted uranium without telling our soldiers, many of whom suffered strange ills, many of whom died mysteriously in ten, 15 years. And Bush and maybe Tony Blair destroyed all the water purification and sewage plants, destroying a chance for clean water. So about a million little kids and babies died, something Osama bin Laden listed as one reason for 9/11. About a half million elderly too, also vulnerable to impure water. But they're not Americans, so who cares?

Well, where are we now? Four years into another Iraq war, 750,000 Iraqis dead, several million gone to nearby lands because of the civil war, constant violence and fear, loss of hope, loss of electricity, loss of lives . . . Iraqis and Americans both. Bush the Younger has sunk in the polls, finally American citizens and even Congress realize that maybe this was just one war too many, huh?

But who will bet that in 10 or 15 years after this nasty little war is over, if another U.S. president decides he wants to go to war with a stubborn little nation thousands of miles away, Congress and the American people will pull out their flags and cheer our innocent young soldiers on their way to, as Eisenhower put it, the "brutality, futility and stupidity of war"?

BARACK OBAMA AND
MORAL JUDGMENT

If Bush is right, and we must fear terrorist acts against us, then we need a change of president.

If Al Gore is right, that we have to worry about serious effects of global warming, then we need a change of president.

If Lou Dobbs is right, that too many of our industries have gone overseas for lower wages and tax breaks, then we need a change in the presidency.

If, as many pundits and media say, our stature in the world is at a historic low, then we need a change of president.

Terrorism is something that, right now, many nations are acquainted with, not just our own. But if Muslims destroyed the Trade Centers in anger, maybe we should consider reasons that impelled them to do this terrible thing, killing three thousand innocent people. Is there ever a valid reason for killing innocent people? In Great Britain, there have been questions about their own possible provocation for such terrorist actions in their country—perhaps, they ask, have they been too repressive, too harsh and critical of the Muslims—their religion, their habits, their industry, their international relationships?

In our country, there has simply been anger, resentment, and with the Afghan and Iraq wars, apparently desire for revenge. But Iraq had nothing to do with our losses on 9/11—so how did our destruction of their country, deaths of a million of their men, women, children and babies, help to lessen anger toward us? Has our war against Iraqis possibly become THEIR 9/Il? Again, is there ever a valid reason for killing innocent people? Like us, will they want to avenge their million dead and many homeless by attacking us and killing many Americans? Are we just lucky that they lack our methods of shipping soldiers and bombs across the seas—to OUR cities and countryside?

Eight wars since the end of WW II have not brought us respect of the world, and have cost us hundreds of thousands of deaths of our young soldiers, too often forced by the Draft to go to war. Of the candidates for president, only Obama, Dennis Kucinich, Ron Paul and Senator Steve Gravel had opposed the Iraq War. Although a great force of Hillary's loyalists assert they will refuse to vote for Obama, they should realize that our Iraq War has brought our country's reputation to rock bottom. And Hillary voted for this war even though she, more than any other senator, must have seen that the men who surrounded the new President Bush in 2000 were the very same men who had asked her husband, President Clinton, to invade Iraq and take out Saddam in 1998—The Project for a New American Century members Donald Rumsfeld, Paul Wolfowitz, Dick Cheney, "Scooter" Libby, Zalmay Khalilzad, Douglas Feith, etc. President Clinton saw no reason then to invade Iraq, nor did many like Senator Ted Kennedy, Robert Byrd and Republican Lincoln Chaffee in 2003.

Was it for Hillary a matter of judgment or a political decision to appear patriotic and support the then popular president for the Iraq War? She of course was not the only one to agree to one more war against a power that had not harmed us in any way—a terrible dictator, yes, but the horror of war, so often condemned by General-President Eisenhower, was not a humanitarian choice. Obama not only saw that, but spoke out forcefully against the war, before it began, in his home state of Illinois even though fiends advised him that it was unwise, would sound unpatriotic. Moral judgment . . . the quality most crucial in a candidate, in anyone, certainly in a president. The Hillary-only Democrats should reflect on the serious issues of life and death, watch those severely injured veterans, read the names and ages of those killed each week that appear on the Lehrer News Hour. Perhaps, even search for the figures of Iraqi dead from our needless war, a war thousands of young American veterans are protesting—if they're still alive.

Which brings us to John McCain, Republican, hawk, maverick most of the time. A vital personality, appearing strong, confident, with humor and a sort of genuineness I used to find admirable. He has the authority of a man who has been in the business of politics a long time, which he has. I don't challenge his age—only his strong support for a war that has destroyed a nation that had not harmed us at all, killed or injured thousands of young Americans, and caused deaths of a million Iraqis and terrified two million of them to leave their homeland.

Yes, he gains great respect for having been a prisoner during the Vietnam War—another needless war, this time waged by a Democratic president, Lyndon Johnson. McCain's trying five years as a prisoner deserve our sympathy, but that war was another mistake—the Vietnamese had not harmed us, and yet our bombs, Agent Orange and Napalm killed 3,200, 000 Vietnamese citizens. It is hard to understand why this experience and the facts of that war have not turned McCain away from war like Republican Eisenhower, not toward it. Eisenhower often spoke out against the "brutality, futility, stupidity of war!"

Other issues of course pertain—earlier somewhat supportive of a Woman's Right to Choose, now McCain is staunchly opposed. He has supported 95 % of Bush's plots and plans, expressed no concern for the nation-wide loss of jobs with no advance in sight due to outsourcing, no concern, with his own and his wife's millions, for those who cannot find enough work to survive and have no health insurance.

McCain's choice of his running mate, the young Sarah Palin, has aroused cheers from fellow Republicans, but Democrats are more realistic. Next in line to the biggest job in the world, she stands articulate, poised and pretty, admitting she "hasn't looked much" at the world-resented Iraq War, but she will no doubt draw a lot of voters opposed to Women's Choice. (Maybe a small problem for some with her young daughter's unmarried pregnancy.) And maybe she will win those epicureans who relish the joys of "moose-burgers."

Al Gore must be right about global warming, since acclaimed scientists agree with him. So does Obama, promising if elected to work with other nations to protect our world more diligently. As for losses of jobs with losses of companies sent overseas, Obama has shown deep concern for this ever since he began working as a law school graduate in the areas of steel plant closings in Chicago. Our country in a historic low with the rest of the world? The war Obama protested is the major reason for such disdain—he will work more closely with the rest of the world to help us climb back up to the higher position we held before President Cheney-Bush crashed our reputation in the streets of Iraq and threw into stark cubicles thousands of untried prisoners to be humiliated and tortured—though George Washington said "We must never use torture!"

There is only one choice for a president who respects human life, cares about the great world around us, the struggle of many Americans to make ends meet and share The American Dream. For Moral Judgment, Barack Obama.

METAPHORS FOR SALE—
WAR ON TERRORISM!

We can spy on our citizens—after all, "We're AT WAR! WAR ON TERRORISM!"

Billions more for the military, when our children are hungry, food stamps being cut—because "We're AT WAR! WAR ON TERRORISM!"

We should pay attention to our citizens' need for healthcare, the high costs of drugs, but these things will have to wait—right now "We're AT WAR—WAR ON TERRORISM!"

Our soldiers are entrapped now in a civil war, let's bring them all home—"No, we can't leave," cry Mr. Bush and Mr. Cheney, because "We're at war—WAR ON TERRORISM!"

Oh, of course, I get it—a METAPHOR! A metaphor like President Johnson's "War on Poverty," searching for ways to END poverty—job programs, job training, etc. And Barbara Bush's "War on Illiteracy." This meant ENDING it by more funds for teachers and tutors, donating books to areas lacking a library, etc. Problems requiring research, effort, hope for solutions.

Then our "War on Terrorism" is just the President's (Rove's) METAPHOR for ENDING terrorism. Requiring research and effort, conferring with other countries that have the same problem—England, Spain, Italy, Turkey, Morocco, Saudi Arabia, etc. How are THEY trying to end terrorism? What have they told you, Bush-Cheney?

Wait now—Johnson's "War on Poverty" didn't mean he wanted to shoot all poor people—Barbara's "War on Illiteracy" didn't mean she wanted to shoot slow readers, kill all of them . . . so why is Bush-Cheney still killing Muslims when we want to have a more peaceable relationship with them?

Isn't that what our government SHOULD be doing—trying to LESSEN terrorism?

But we have thousands of actual soldiers in Iraq—yeah, that's because we DID wage a real war against Iraq—not because of terrorism, no, because of its weapons of mass destruction, its development of nuclear—uh, well, no, Saddam did NOT have WMD, and WASN'T getting nuclear tubes from Niger. And both the president and then Secretary of Defense Rtumsfeld said that they have "no evidence that Saddam had any connection to 9/11."

Just the same, President Bush says he would have gone to war anyway, without these reasons, "Because we're safer, the whole world is safer with Saddam gone!"

Well, we can all see that, all right. The Iraqis, afraid to walk down the street for fear of being shot, kidnapped, robbed, or if a woman, being raped, might have a little trouble seeing that. Even American contractors and reporters working in Iraq might have a little trouble seeing that—so many of their co-workers have been killed. Kind of bleary, discerning the REAL war from the metaphoric "WAR on TERRORISM!"

So, what's the story here? Some have said that war IS terrorism—the killing of innocents. Reliable news sources say that since our war, Iraq has become a magnet for terrorists intent on killing American soldiers and workers. "You kill a Muslim in Iraq, you kill my brother!" cried a Muslim from Spain on NPR radio. If we stay there and keep killing people, not knowing if they're innocent citizens, terrorists, insurgents or what, when will we know we've killed all of the real terrorists and have ended our "WAR ON TERRORISM"?

And those other countries that have suffered acts of terrorism too—are they also trying to end radical Muslim terrorism against them by daily killing of Muslims? Not that we've heard. If, as Bush often claims, his first concern is making the American people secure, is he accomplishing this by LESSENING terrorism? How? He was so incensed by the bombing of our Trade Centers and deaths of almost 3,000 Americans that in retaliation he bombed heavily in Afghanistan trying to strike down the man who was allegedly responsible, Osama bin Laden, killing 1600 Afghans, mostly innocents. How incensed may the Iraqi Muslims be at Bush-Cheney's destruction of their nation, frightening two million citizens out of their homeland, and causing deaths of now said to be close to a million Iraqis?

Every day we are there in Iraq, killing, destroying, frightening Iraq Muslims, are we LESSENING incentives for terrorism or INCREASING them?

Isn't it time to set up a quick commission to delve into the causes of "terrorism"? Osama has stated openly that one reason for his 9/11 attack was deaths of a million children from impure water caused by Gulf War One's destruction of water purification plants and 10 years of sanctions (Bush One and Clinton) forbidding import of chlorine to purify their water. Is this worth noting? Why has refusing to let Iraq purify its water been something of a secret? Osama's second reason for his attack was our defense of Israel in denying rights to Muslim Palestine; the third our presence of military might near holy sites in Saudi Arabia, now withdrawn.

If there is deep resentment and anger at our unfailing support for Israel and indifference to the suffering of Palestinians—Muslims—under the restrictive policies of Israel, shouldn't we look very seriously into this since it seems to be one basis for hatred and violence—terrorism—against us? If the president's top priority is the safety of the American people—then why not convene a group to study this crucial problem? How can we risk continuing anger with likelihood of retaliation from a large segment of the Muslim population?

When Helen Thomas asked Mr. Bush why he went to war in Iraq since they had no WMD's or nuclear connection, Mr. Bush said solemnly, "No president wants to go to war, but you see, Helen, everything has changed since 9'11!" And then, said the President, "We're at war—WAR ON TERRORISM!"

"WAR ON TERRORISM" is a metaphor. How long will we let our young, life-loving soldiers die for a metaphor?

NOW, SPEAKING OF PEACE . . .

General and Republican President of the United States, Dwight Eisenhower: "I hate war as only a man who has been there can, who has seen its brutality, its futility, its stupidity!

Every gun that's made, every warship launched, every rocket fired signifies, in the final sense, a theft from those who hunger and are not fed, those who are cold and are not clothed. The world in arms is not spending alone; it is spending the sweat of its laborers, the genius of its scientists, the hopes of its children. This is not a way of life at all, in any true sense. Under the cloud of threatening war, it is humanity hanging from an iron cross!"

George W. Bush: "We're bringing peace to Iraq, peace to the Middle East."

Confucius: "We cannot use war as an instrument to bring peace."

Bertrand Russell: War does not determine who is right, only who is left.

Ralph Bunche: Thee are no warlike people, just warlike leaders.

Albert Einstein: It is characteristic of the military mentality that non-human factors—atom bombs, weapons of all sorts—are held essential while the human being, his desires and thoughts, are considered as unimportant and secondary, as merely human material.

President Dwight "Ike" Eisenhower: Beware the military-industrial complex.

Croesus: In peace, the sons bury their fathers, but in war, the fathers bury their sons.

Dr. Martin Luther King: Our scientific power has outrun our spiritual power. We have guided missiles and misguided men. Love is the only force capable of turning an enemy into a friend.

Abraham Lincoln: The best way to destroy an enemy is to make him into a friend.

Mohandas Gandhi: I object to violence, because when it appears to do good, the good is only temporary, the evil it does is permanent.

Salvador Dali: Wars never hurt anybody except the people who die.

Henry Fosdick: The tragedy of war is that it uses man's best to do man's worst.

IRAQ MAN who lost 6 of his family, from my play, "A New War, Anyone?" Based on a man shown on CNN early in the Iraq War; most of the words are his.

Abbrahim: I don't know you Americans, once I thought you were good people, helping poor countries . . . but now, how can I feel—when you have killed six members of my family! In your bombs!

At first I thought you were going to capture Saddam Hussein, a very bad man, yes, but I never came near him, never saw him, he never hurt me, and the country was—was at peace, my wife could walk out at night, and my children play outside in the sunshine and I did not worry about them . . . and now—they are all dead! Your terrible planes came over my house—and they poured fire and smoke on my house, and destroyed it! My family was sleeping, while I was away—and when I came home the next morning—I had no home! No wife! My five children all dead! Buried in the rubble that was now my home! I had to dig out my family—my little daughter, she was so pretty and so smart, just 6 years old—Dig them all out of the debris with my bare hands—and then I had to bury them all—with my bare hands!

You, George Bush—you have ruined my life—what did we Iraqi people ever do to you, that you would do such a thing to us, to me? Nothing! Even Saddam—he did nothing to you! But now, now that you have killed so many of my family, should we go into your country as you have done here, and kill thousands of your people? You and your high level men—you should be tried for mass murder—of my wife, my wife of 22 years, and five innocent little children all dead—how can I go on living! (He sobs)

You claim to be a religious man who prays to God—my God will not listen to you!

You are a man of evil and hard heart! Sitting safe and cheerful in your big White House, you order the horror and death of people who have done you no harm! God will not forgive you, George Bush! Never! Never!

IRAQ DOCTOR SPEAKS OUT

Doctor: I am exhausted . . . three days without sleep, all of us here, trying to save lives . . . since you Americans attacked Baghdad in such a shocking series of horrific bombing, we have been receiving more than a hundred wounded every day . . . without enough beds for them, without enough medicines—not enough surgeons to save them! So yes, they are dying!

Do you Americans know this? Do you care? Of course we are receiving some of your soldiers too, crying in pain and agony! Why this war on us—again? Wasn't it enough that after the first Gulf War you bombed and destroyed our water facilities, water purification plants so we had no pure water—and then held those sanctions against us that prohibited us from getting material to purify our water? Do you know that more than a half million children, babies and elderly, so vulnerable to poor water—have died because of those cruel sanctions you and England enforced for 12 years! More than a half million! And now another war to shock and kill us?

Yes, you lost 3000 people in the attack on your Trade Towers—terrible! But that had nothing to do with me or my patients or with Iraq—nothing to do with the two little boys who were burned in your big bombs—one ten, one 12 years old—burned on their bodies so deeply that their nerves were destroyed and they could not feel the pain—and they both died a few days later!

I invite your president Bush to come here to visit and see just what his bombs and missiles have done—to innocent people, men, women and children, babies. Such cruelty as he has never experienced. I must go, new wounded are screaming and crying . . .

BISHOP THOMAS GUMBLETON, OF DETROIT

Against our war, against all wars

"War is wrong," says Catholic Bishop Thomas Gumbleton, world traveler, advocate of peace, justice and human rights for all people.

"I believe with President John Kennedy, that we must end war, or war will end us! The weapons used today, anti-personnel weapons, are aimed at whole populations—who gets killed? The ordinary people."

And he has been acquainted with war, our present war. Astonishingly, he has been to Iraq nine times, the last visit in 2004, a year after Bush-Cheney's war began. But he'd been there after the first Gulf war of Bush One. "The people of Iraq have been in agony since 1991—that first war destroyed so much of their infrastructure, water purification plants, so much they depended on for their daily lives, food and clean water. They've been living in poverty since then."

The bishop, nationally known for his Jesus-like compassion for the poor, the mistreated and suffering around the world, speaks with a gentle, unhesitating calm. Referring to his last visit to Iraq in 2004, he recalled that "It was a terrible time for the people, bombing, and so many kidnappings." As for how the government we set up is working, he simply noted that "Today more Sunni members of their government resigned—the government is unraveling." While the Shi'ia majority decided to go on a summer vacation, heat neared 130, our soldiers blistering under 100 pounds of protective armor.

"Bush had no understanding before the war began of the different factions there, historical differences." The bishop speaks like both a dedicated Christian and an historian. As things stand now, the Bishop cites the problems in Northern Ireland with England. "They were killing each other until they finally began talking to each other, and they achieved peace. The groups in Iraq need to do the same thing, realize their differences and the situation they are in.

"Our presence there is bringing more suffering, more violence, so many deaths each day."

What is the solution for what is broadly called this "quagmire"?

"We have to leave—while we're there protecting the Shi'ia-run government because we want this domination, there's no chance for the different factions to settle their differences. But if we leave, they will have to solve their problems themselves; they will in time, as has happened in other places."

Why do the American people accept our many wars, do not seem to be concerned about the stress and thousands of deaths of the Iraqi people?

"They don't know them, have never been there. If the media showed more of the Iraqi people being injured and being killed, the reality of their life now, they would react differently."

He himself speaks with despair of the years of suffering for the Iraqi people from both of our wars and our sanctions. "Some of my friends, many people I knew there have been killed, 3,000 dying each month. And Bush has no strategic plan for ending the war."

Bishop Gumbleton noted the troubled history of Iraq, created by the British in the 1920's. "In the 1950s, Iraq overthrew a CIA agent we supported, but we kept him there until 1958 when we put in a minority leader who became our puppet. When Saddam came into power in 1979, we were friendly with him until Gulf War One, and finally he was removed by our second Gulf War."

I mentioned that since World War II only two of our presidents had no wars, Jimmy Carter and General-President Eisenhower, who often said how he hated war. "Yes," the Bishop concurred, "but Eisenhower had two coups, one in Guatemala and one in Iran. We took out Iran's elected leader Mossadegh in 1953. You can see why they don't like us."

"Bush says that Al Qaeda's center is in Iraq, but it's not under supervision there. Bush has no sense of reality—we must look beyond Iraq, into other international groups. The threat is not in Iraq, it's mired in Islamist extremism, and we need to form a political global alliance, world-wide, with long objectives well outside Iraq." Regretting our frequent way of settling problems with war, Bishop Gumbleton insists we need to use "diplomacy and economic methods of working out problems."

He mentions the billions spent on guns and weapons that could be better used for helping people in trouble and suffering.

And he questions the oft-mentioned "War on terrorism." "Acts of violence in England are treated not as 'terrorism,' but as 'crimes', which they are, and the British have arrested some of those who have committed such crimes. This is more effective than waging war, 'war on terrorism,' as Bush calls it."

The Bishop, now in his seventies, has traveled the world to offer help and sympathy to those under stress, often to Central and South American countries such as Nicaragua and El Salvador, also often to Haiti, recalling our kidnapping of their famed leader Aristide and taking him without any questioning to Africa. "To Chad, but now he's in South Africa teaching at a university, and waiting to give a chance to Haiti's new government." The Bishop, who was there recently, says "conditions are a little better now."

This bishop is a "man for all seasons" entrenched in efforts for peace and humanity all around our world. Our leaders would be wise to listen to him.

METHODIST BISHOPS REGRET LACK OF EARLY WAR PROTEST

"War Turns Us into the Evil We Fear"
—*Bishop Joe Wilson*

He has spoken out since before the Iraq War began, spoken out against all wars, but retired Texas Bishop Joe Wilson feels pangs of regret that the full body of Methodist bishops failed to protest forcefully before he war began. "This is why we issued a Statement of Conscience, signed by 110 of our bishops, expressing our feelings about this war. But before our nation's rush to action in another war, too many were quiet. Now we repent of our complicity—we were not strong enough before the war started."

The home of President George W. Bush in Crawford, Texas, was within his area of religious leadership. "I was sympathetic with Cindy Sheehan, and held a church service for her and the folks with her near Crawford." Bishop Wilson speaks gently, softly, but firm in his belief that religious members "must be Christian peacekeepers 'To kill or be killed' is a betrayal of our scriptures." Over and over, Bishop Wilson returned to the teachings of Jesus. "We belong to one another, to those of other cultures. We hold a kinship with all others created by God. If you look at some of the world as enemies, you have no pain in their destruction . . . Jesus Christ taught differently."

Mentioning the many persons held in our prisons for detainees, he spoke critically of their treatment, "our use of torture. We become what we hate. War turns us into the evil we fear." The Bishop recited the rate of gradual increases in civilian deaths through the world's many wars. In World War One, levels of civilian deaths were low because the soldiers fought in designated trenches. Recent wars have heightened the civilian deaths—war in the 1980's, 74% civilian deaths; in the 1990's, 90% civilian deaths. No figures for the new century's wars, but so far we know that civilian Iraqi deaths in our invasion numbered 100,000, more than Iraq soldiers since their soldiers had not yet been involved. With the civil war there now, numbers of deaths have risen to more than 750,000." Bishop Wilson quoted the anti-war minister of Riverside Church in New York City, William Sloane Coffin, who died last year, in discussing religious leaders protesting: "They become like politicians, so cautious they become moral failures."

Bishop Wilson is not a moral failure, steadfast in his belief that the Christian tradition does not include the killing of innocents in war. So why do we Americans have so many wars? "These terrible weapons are made by large, wealthy interests whose purpose is to make the rich richer, and our government lacks the boldness to stand against this power—so against the Christian tradition."

Because other bishops also felt deep regret at not speaking out sooner against the war, they issued "A Call to Repentance and Peace with Justice," beginning "As followers of Jesus Christ, who named peacemakers as Children of God," they wrote: "As elected and consecrated bishops of the Church, we repent of our complicity in what we believe to be the unjust and immoral invasion and occupation of Iraq . . . in the U.S. administration's rush toward military action based on misleading information, too many of us were silent . . . while American men and women are sent to Iraq to kill and be killed, while thousands of Iraqi people needlessly suffer and die, while poverty increases and preventable diseases go untreated . . . Although we value the sacrifices of the men and women who serve in the military, we confess our betrayal of the scriptural and prophetic authority to warn the nations that true security lies not in weapons of war, but in enabling the poor, the vulnerable, the marginalized to flourish as the beloved daughters and sons of God." They urge their churches toward "peacemaking . . . working for the things that make for peace: personal, institutional, and governmental priorities that protect the poor and most vulnerable; an end to prejudice toward people of other faiths and cultures, confronting differences and conflicts with humility, dialogue and respect without being so cautious in confronting evil that we lose out moral authority."

Again and again, in considering the teachings of varied religions, the word "moral, morality . . ." a final message of these bishops that should be far reaching: "Let us move beyond caution rooted in self protection and recover moral authority anchored in commitment to Jesus Christ, the Prince of Peace."

PRAYER FOR PEACE

We pray, we plea, we work for peace,
We pray, we plea to value life,
The mystery, complexity, beauty
of each human life.
We aspire to preserve life, all lives,
So our soldiers, new to life,
Can live to develop their dreams,
Their hopes, their talents, explore
this beautiful world
As we, far from the terror of war's madness,
can live our lives.
And we pray, we plea, for the lives of those
We cannot know, in lands far away
Where daily tasks and pleasures
Are shrouded in fear of our mindless bombs.
So we strive to guide our nation
Into a world of patient kindness
Toward all countries, where words and hopes
Are shared, in all times,
forever replacing war,
forever replacing war.

PROFITS, PATRIOTISM AND WAR

As long ago as the years just following World War One, called "The War to End All Wars," leaders hoped for an end to future wars, yet worried about the interests that fostered wars.

President Woodrow Wilson, not a raving radical, said, "The U.S. government is a foster child of the special interests." Although not tying in his thoughts to war, Abraham Lincoln, not a raving radical, said: "Corporations have been enthroned—the money power will endeavor to prolong its reign until all wealth is aggregated in a few hands and the republic is destroyed."

Derrick Jackson, Boston Globe columnist, in 2003: "The average pay of a soldier in Iraq is $20,000 a year; the average pay of defense contractors, 577 times that, on average $11.3 million. Each year of the Iraq War, CEO pay rises—Lockheed Martin, in two years from 5.8 million to 25.3 million. At Honeywell aircraft systems, from 12.9 million to 45 million."

But early in World War II, President Roosevelt said: "A common sense of decency makes it imperative that no new group of war millionaires shall come into being in this nation as a result of struggles abroad. The American people will not relish the idea of any American citizen growing rich and fat in an emergency of blood and slaughter and human suffering." But 63 years after Roosevelt's speech, a new group of war millionaires came into being, both as a result of America's struggle abroad and its abandonment of the human struggle at home.

After World War One, leaders hoped for a successful drive against war, and for international peace. President Wilson felt, however, that the control of government had "slipped into the hands of the combined manufacturers and financiers, whose interests too often are linked with imperialism and militarism."

Similarly, General-Republican-Twice President Dwight Eisenhower, not a raving radical, warned fervently about the threats to our nation of the Military-Industrial-Complex that could spend billions of our dollars on military hardware, horrendous bombs and missiles to keep wars going for profits, depriving "food for those who are hungry," and clothing "for those who are cold and not clothed."

Republican President Herbert Hoover, not a raving radical, said after World War One, in an Armistice Day speech given in 1931: "A solemn obligation lies upon us to press forward in our pursuit of those things for which they (soldiers) died. Our duty is to . . . insure the world against the horror and wastage of war." During his years in office, days of the great Depression, he said "Our current expenditures on military constitute the largest military budget of any nation on earth . . ." James Shotwell, then of the Carnegie Endowment for Peace, said "In this year of economic depression, the world is spending 4 to 5 billions in preparation for the next war." Bertrand Russell, in his book "Why Men Fight," declares that "Patriotism, like the ancient religions, seems to demand its persecutions, its holocausts. Its lurid heroic cruelties; like them, it is noble, primitive, brutal and mad!"

After World War One there was more thought expressed about ending wars than today when our weaponry is so much more powerful and deadly. Early in the last century, Republican Senator Charles Sumner of New England said: "Not that I love my country less, but Humanity more, do I now and here plead the cause of a higher and truer patriotism. I cannot forget that we are men by a more sacred bond than we are citizens—that we are children of a common Father more than we are Americans."

Almost a hundred years ago many clergy and politicians worried about dangers of the munitions makers, tied to Eisenhower's "Military Industrial Complex." A minister after World War One, Dr. Charles Jefferson, of the Great Broadway Church, asserted, "We must go to work with fresh vigor to bring about a reduction in armament, for it matters little what you say on paper so long as you build cruisers, bombs and manufacture poison gas. If the ideals of Jesus are right, then the ideals of the militarist are wrong. These annual war games on land and sea and in the air tear all of our peace resolutions into shreds. All this makes Christianity a mockery . . ."

Here a potent statement: "Most people want peace until their passions are inflamed and their fears aroused by fantastic stories about trumped up dangers. Who arouses these passions and fears? The war makers—those who in their bitter international rivalry for markets, raw materials and fields of investment enlist the aid of battleships and soldiers . . . for colonies, oil fields, coal mines, trade routes. Behind competitive armament lies economic competition as its cause."

Does this sound like President Eisenhower warning about the Military Industrial Complex after World War II? But the words are of Reverend Herman J. Hahn, pastor of the Salem Evangelical Synod Church in Buffalo, New York, urging peace after World War One. We have come a long way in time, but the road is familiar.

Rev. Hahn, a friend of Norman Thomas and Professor-Reverend Reinhold Niebuhr, was condemning reasons for World War One, ten wars ago for our nation. "War is a stubborn foe," he declared in a series of radio addresses, "entrenched in our economies, politics, education, religion and psychology. Not through pretty phrases will we destroy war, but determined, aggressive, courageous action on the Christian front . . . to keep faith with the soldiers who have died in Flanders Field. This it means to be loyal to Him who died as Prince of Peace on the cross—this it means to be true to our nation that has solemnly outlawed war."

Those early leaders would have been horrified at our accepted killing of 3,200,000 innocent fellow human beings in our Vietnam War, as at our destruction of a Muslim nation, Iraq, with many times the toll in human life as in the limited trenches of World War One.

Across these many years of wars for no reason, these men have spoken out passionately for peace. Lincoln and Wilson and Hoover and Kennedy and Eisenhower and Roosevelt and Jimmy Carter and so many more, in churches and in Washington, have struggled to turn us away from war and toward a humane congeniality with all of the world's peoples.

THE ADVANCE OF CIVILIZATION

Ah, how far we all have come
In the advance of civilization.
All nations, touching ours
or at the farthest shores,
are in our family,
speaking to us and we to them,
sharing inventions and ideas,
poems, recipes, food and bombs;
families separated by a thousand miles
speaking as if next door,
by telegram, then telephone,
now the magic of e-mail.
Oh, the wonders of our scientific advances!
Once days of sailing on unrushed ships,
Now the cleverness of planes that whip
Through the clouds like eagles
with magical powers, fearless as night.
Planes, cars with speed of light,
Yes, cars, planes, computers, cell phones,
E mail, I-pods and bombs.
Civilization marches on!

The world at large, all nations
Dashing forward in the world's advance,
Sharing our miracles, medicines and bombs,
Saving lives once destined to death,
But now new breath from the brilliance,
The dedication of scientists
who labor long, tirelessly to find
the formula to save a million lives,
or when our leaders so command,
to kill a million more.

DEMOCRATS NOW LEADING CONGRESS—STOP THE MADNESS IN IRAQ!

WE'RE CREATING TERRORISTS!

Our Number One fear—Terrorism!

And we are inspiring new terrorists every day we stay in Iraq—we invaders, occupiers, killers of innocents, destroyers of homes and cities as we trample on the roots of our civilization. Is this hard to see, Congress?

What are you waiting for? Not even a tough-worded Censure for Bush and Cheney? The more civilized people of the world who respect human life and deplore our many barbaric wars—they're waiting for your action! Those who live in shadowed fear that THEY might be our next target—they're waiting anxiously for your action!

Our American cousins in Central and South America are waiting to see if at long last you Democrats in a terrible war time will see that your country must end its constant military interference in their lands—so will you take some action? At least SAY something?

Thousands of us in this country who opposed our latest war—our 8th since World War II—we're growing angry and impatient waiting for your action. Do SOMEthing!

The blind eyes of the president and vice-president can't see an obvious fact—we are hated OCCUPIERS! We won the war in a few weeks—Mission Accomplished! But the Occupation? MISSION FAILED! If some giant bomb-tossing power had attacked us, had destroyed blocks of homes around you, crushing thousands of children and their mothers and fathers, grandmothers to death, wouldn't you want them and their ghastly killing machines out of YOUR home towns? If they wouldn't leave Dayton or Portland or Cleveland, wouldn't some of our young men be attacking these occupiers who had killed their loved ones? An Iraqi woman on NPR said they want our soldiers out NOW!

What of the president and vice-president's constant mantra—"War on terrorism"?

It's a METAPHOR, for God's sake—don't let them get away with it! Don't let our young soldiers keep dying for a METAPHOR! Keep saying this so it gets on our TV sets!

Because the longer we stay, more Muslims will be infuriated and charge into violence against us—they can't reach the White House to punish Cheney and Bush for killing and mutilating their families and fellow Muslims, but they'll attack and kill whomever they can to show their anti-American rage—our soldiers! We all know that a wild civil war is adding to our destruction and killing there, but how can we help when we started the whole thing? We're not problem-solvers! Ask the U.N. to organize a respected committee to meet with the varied factions—Nelson Mandela, Desmond Tutu, Jimmy Carter, other Middle East leaders.

Democrats—we know your majority is small, but you can at least speak out LOUDLY—insist that our media be allowed to show photographs of our dead soldiers, returning body bags, and bodies of Iraqi babies and children killed by our soldiers. Patriotism must allow truth to be seen and told. Why should only mothers and fathers of our dead soldiers see their bodies? Why not the rest of us? Why not our president and vice-president?

Some of our soldiers are speaking out and refusing to return to Iraq, thousands deserting, more than a hundred committing suicide rather than return to the horror. Former generals are speaking out against the war—but what can they do now? But you in Congress, you Democrats and more and more Republicans appalled by our shameful presence in a country that had done us no harm—what are you DOING? What are you SAYING now that you have the limelight on C-Span?

Cut off the funds! That's what finally ended the shameful Vietnam War. Cancel the horribly expensive war contracts for the too-powerful Military Industrial Complex that General-President Eisenhower warned us about. Terminate further development of atomic might when we already have more than enough nuclear bombs to destroy the world—and planning to send this terrible power into outer space!

Insist on knowing EVERY PLACE in the world where your government is holding persons suspected of terrorism—and that every detainee know the charges against him and is represented by a lawyer to prove or disprove those charges, being true to our Constitution and the Geneva Accords, erasing the world-viewed disgrace of incarceration without evidence or trial. This is NOT the American way of justice—not until Bush-Cheney! Our Constitution states that YOU—CONGRESS—are in charge of all "captures on Land and on Waters!" Where have you been?

Yes, Iraq is in horrific condition, and many of you may feel that we can't leave because we're responsible. Of course we are. But the Iraqi woman on NPR said that our presence is bringing in more and more insurgents from other places who add to the violence. Polls of Iraqis show that a majority of them do want us to leave—we the occupiers who caused their debacle, their fears, their losses of family, friends, doctors, teachers, the peaceable life they once had when children could walk to school and women walk down the street without fear of being shot, raped, robbed or kidnapped.

And now Bush-Cheney is devious about their approach to Iran, further worrying and infuriating the Muslim world, provoking more grounds for revenge against us—TERRORISM! What are you doing about this, Congress? Why not firm action FORBIDDING use of military force in Iran? With STRONG PROTESTING VOICES!

And when are you leaders going to set up a commission to ascertain the REAL ways to lessen terrorism? Surely you don't think more and more killing of Muslims will DIMINISH Muslim hatred toward us and desire for retaliation—terrorism!

Cheney-Bush-Rumsfeld-Wolfowitz has proved an axis of evil, brought deaths to MORE Americans—more than 3,800 young American soldiers—than the 3,000 lost on 9/11—Point this out! The President insists they must stay indefinitely so more and more will die. In our invasion we killed more than 100,000 innocent Iraqis, and the civil war we paved the way for has hiked the toll to more than 855,000. The Muslims and radical Muslims see this. The world sees this!

Surely some of you do. You lawmakers have the public eye—show how the President's talk of "resolve" and "stay the course" and "our values" are easy for him to say, but mean more DEAD young Americans!

All of you in Congress, like Kennedy and Chuck Hagel and Dennis Kucinich and Ron Paul, must recognize a frightening fact—your president and vice-president possess not a drop of human feeling over deaths of innocent Iraqis or Americans. If they had, they never would have begun this war—.remember, Cheney-Runsfeld-Wolfowitz and friends asked Clinton in 1998 to invade Iraq and take out Saddam, well before 9/11, later asserting it would be a cakewalk.

The ever-watching world must see that such carnage is held accountable—by impeachment. If you leaders in Congress accept these inhuman crimes, what can the world's citizens conclude? Probably you can't get the total votes to effect impeachment—but at least demonstrate verbally that you will TRY for it—set up issues of impeachment and let your voices of righteous anger be HEARD! Enough of RESTRAINT!

Surely after eight wars since World War II, something must be done to contemplate our country's future—terrorism fears demand this. The deaths of 3,800 young, healthy American soldiers demand this. The tragic losses and chaos in Iraq that has sent more than two million Iraqis to other lands demand this. Hope of restoring our international image demands this.

Democrats, you're in the spotlight—puncture the president's empty rhetoric—when he says that the persons who bombed in the Green Zone—"They don't care anything about killing innocent people!" ask him how HE feels about killing hundreds of THOUSANDS of innocent people! Good heavens—TALK BACK!

Congress—don't be Shy! Stop the terrorist-recruiting madness in Iraq! NOW!

WE DON'T CARE MUCH ABOUT HUMAN LIFE, IN MANY WAYS

It's a strong indictment, but true: As a nation, we don't care much about human life. This cannot be questioned when we consider that we have waged eight—yes, 8—needless wars since World War II. More than any other nation. Yet President Bush has said about other nations, "They don't respect human lives as we do . . ." Give him credit for chutzpah!

Our president opposes Iraq's plan to grant amnesty to Iraqis who have killed American soldiers. As evidenced since the North Korean and Vietnam wars, we seem to believe we have the right to invade any country, even a country that has done us no harm at all, and kill thousands, or as in Vietnam even 3,200,000 human beings, with no sense of guilt or regret.

Attach a cloak of patriotism to a president's wish for war, Congress and enough of the public say okay, ignoring the Constitution's rule that only Congress may declare war, and realizing that thousands of our very young, hopeful citizens will be killed or have their arms and legs torn off, their minds damaged beyond cure. Human lives lost, mothers, fathers, spouses, friends anguished. Europe now has a Union to settle problems diplomatically, avoiding war as urged by President Roosevelt, British Winston Churchill, and General and Republican President Eisenhower. But we don't revere human life as those countries do.

We watch the rest of the developed world provide health care for all of their citizens and stand by, the wealthiest nation in the history of the world, and let millions struggle desperately for medical help. While in most other nations the cost of a new drug is determined fairly by the government, here a pharmaceutical company can set its own price, often too costly for lower income citizens. An elderly friend, whose extreme pain was relieved by only a certain drug denied by her Medicare provider, suffered intensely until her Congressman intervened.

Even Saddam Hussein had health care for his citizens. Our government just doesn't care.

A woman in her thirties appeared on a TV show recently to say that by the time she finishes paying off her college loans she will have paid a half million dollars. Again, we lag behind most of the developed world in concern about educating our young. The wealthy have no trouble with soaring college costs, some students get help from their parents, and some cannot attain higher education because of their family's lack of funds.

Sorry to bring this name up again, but even Saddam offered students free college education. So do the countries of Europe, many in the Middle East and South America. But our government doesn't care enough.

Deaths by guns in our country have risen to more than 31,000 a year, mostly of youths in their teens and early twenties, mostly in the poorer areas of cities, mostly in minority populations, African American or those who have immigrated from the far and Middle East. Michigan now suffers more than 1,000 gun deaths each year. In the four years of the Iraq War, more than 3,850 young American soldiers have died. On our streets and in our homes in these same four years, more than 121,000 Americans have been killed by guns.

Too bad for those poor people who can't move to safer places, but Congress and the National Rifle Association just don't care enough. Many other nations have similar minorities, similarly poor, uneducated, angry and disruptive, but there's one difference—those young people cannot get their hands on guns. In Europe and Great Britain, when a person applies for the right to buy a gun, usually at a police station, he must wait months, maybe even a year or more, and then is given permission for—a rifle for hunting! No hand guns, no machine guns.

A few in Congress have tried to pass laws to limit gun sales, but the National Rifle Association donates to so many lawmakers that it seems hopeless. Parents in endangered areas live with fear of gunfire every day, every night, and sooner or later young men are wounded or killed, and small children in the line of fire also. A child in Boston playing with a little cousin grabbed a gun nearby to use in playing, and shot the cousin dead, an accident he will live with the rest of his life. An older relative, just a teenager, was blamed for owning the gun—but why is any young person allowed to buy a thing as murderous as a gun? Only in this country. If a majority of Congressmen and Senators were moved by these daily tragedies, they would pass laws to protect their citizens as do other countries, but they just don't care enough.

When Scotland and Australia suffered school tragedies such as our Columbine and Virginia Tech, they immediately went to work to pass laws preventing further such actions by guns. But our leaders just don't care as much.

Our factories, energy bases, lethal military hardware and medical facilities' toxic wastes are a problem—where to dump them? Somewhere perhaps buried deep in an unpopulated region in a state with wide expanse of desert or mountain to be sure there could be no harmful effects on the health of our citizens, children and babies, certainly the most vulnerable? But no, toxic waste dumps are allowed in cities and towns close by homes, schools, churches, so that thousands are killed or given serious ills by the deadly fumes.

How can this fatal condition exist in our democracy? Because our leaders just don't care enough about the life and death of our poorest, often minority citizens who die from cancer at 20 or 30 due to their proximity to the poisonous dumps.

That we still maintain the death penalty in most of our states is shocking to most of the world that have given up this barbaric action. President Bush, who claims to be a very religious man whose whole life changed when "I took Jesus into my heart" must have heard that the Bible says, "Thou shalt not kill." Yet when he was governor of Texas, and since then, his state has put to death more human beings than any other state.

Of course some crimes are of such cruelty that the perpetrator must be held from society to protect the population. But killing a human being is as wrong for a government as for a citizen. All of Europe has given up such barbaric offenses; no nation may join the European Union if it still retains the death penalty, such is the Union members' strength of conviction. It has been proven that we have at times convicted and put to death a man later proved innocent. Often there is some doubt about the person's guilt, but he or she is killed anyway. We have to become more civilized than this—Congress must pass a law forbidding the death penalty in any state.

The loss of young lives is tragic, needless; neglect of our elderly, poor, ill and troubled a national shame. But as a nation, the richest in the world, we just don't care enough.

There is always hope . . . but not real chances until we find and elect men and women who care deeply about their fellow human beings, here and all around our world.

PRESIDENTIAL QUOTES THAT DEFY BELIEF—AND NEED QUESTIONING

Here's How the Media SHOULD be Responding

Pres. Bush: I'm bringing peace to Iraq.

Media: Aw, c'mon, Mr. President—you're bringing WAR to Iraq—soldiers bombing civilian homes and streets, soldiers shooting people, people killing our soldiers—your bombs have killed 700,000 Iraqis, and you paved the way for another war—their CIVIL WAR!

Pres. Bush: I'm not going to lose my resolve!

Media: Wait a minute—you mean that our fearful, war-weary, three-tours-in-Iraq soldiers have to hang onto THEIR resolve no matter how scared, how dead they are!

Pres. Bush: We're not going to leave until the Job is Done!

Media: Okay, and just what will signify that "the job is done"? Just what defines the "job"?

Pres. Bush: I'm going to Stay The Course!

Media: But what does "The Course" mean? Point it out on this map.

Pres. Bush: I'm bringing democracy to Iraq, bringing democracy to the Middle East!

Media: Not that we've noticed—Maliki isn't being very DEMOCRATIC in how he's dealing with equal rights for all of his citizens—even for the Sunnis. Maybe the Middle East just doesn't like having your kind of democracy shoved down its throat, especially at the point of guns and the deadly power of your missiles and bombs.

Pres. Bush: We're building democracies over there, because democracies don't have as many wars as other kinds of governments.

Media: Are you kidding? Your democracy, the U.S.A., has started more wars than any other country in the past 50 years—eight wars since WWII: North Korea, Vietnam, Grenada, Nicaragua Contra War, Panama Invasion, First Gulf War, Afghan War, second Iraq War. No other country—autocracy, kingdom, dictatorship, whatever—has had as many wars. Jimmy Carter said we're known as the "War Monger of the world."

Pres. Bush: With Saddam gone, we're safer, the world is safer.

Media: Good try. Iraq is a battle zone, citizens can't walk down their streets for fear of being killed, kidnapped, robbed. Two million Iraqis have left their homeland out of fear. Only our heavily protected Green Zone is safe, and even it was recently bombed. Ask any of us how safe we feel there. With anger toward us for the horror we've caused these Muslims, we all have more to fear now.

Pres. Bush: That attack in the Green Zone—they don't feel anything about killing innocent people!

Media: How about you? Do you "feel anything" about the 700,000 innocent people you've killed there, women, men, children, in your bombing? And now 855,000 and adding, killed in the civil war you paved the way for? Some estimates now over a million.

Pres. Bush: The people of Iraq are better off now, they have freedom, they voted for their new democratic government!

Media: Maybe you haven't heard the latest news, since you don't read the papers or watch news programs—they now have Civil War. Remember, you heard it here first! The only Iraqis who feel free now are the millions who have gone to neighboring countries.

Pres. Bush: We don't allow torture, I never have ordered torture.

Media: Really? Then how come so many men, 300 now declared innocent of any anti-American activities and released, are writing articles and books about how brutally they were tortured in our own detainee camps or in "renditions" to countries such as Egypt, Morocco and Syria where torture is routine? Waterboarding still being debated, not declared unlawful?

Pres. Bush: No president wants to go to war, but everything has changed since 9/11, see.

Media: But 9/11 had nothing to do with Saddam Hussein and Iraq, you and Secretary Rumsfeld said this several times. As your former Secretary of the Treasury Paul O'Neill said, as soon as Rumsfeld, Cheney and Wolfowitz came into power with you, they spoke eagerly of war with Iraq, well before 9/11. They and their Project for a New American Century had wanted this war since they asked President Clinton to invade Iraq and take out Saddam in 1998. You gave them the war they wanted, and now you're stuck with it.

Pres. Bush: That Ahmadinejad of Iran, he's the greatest force for terrorism in the Middle East, and Iran is sending weapons into Iraq that are killing our soldiers!

Media: What are your soldiers doing in Iraq? They've killed thousands of Iraqis, destroyed the whole nation so that two million have fled in terror from their homeland.

Iran is more afraid of us, since we took out their elected leader, Mossadegh, in 1954, and we helped Saddam Hussein in his war against Iran in the 1980's by giving him lots of lethal stuff to kill Iranians. What have they ever done to hurt us?

Pres. Bush: We're at war, war on terrorism! We won't leave until we've won this war!

Media: War on Terrorism is a metaphor, like Lyndon Johnson's "War on Poverty," Barbara Bush's "War on Illiteracy." They sought ways to END poverty, END illiteracy, consulting with experts in those fields. Are you consulting experts for the best ways of ending terrorism? Is killing more and more Muslims a way of winning their support against terrorism, or is it provoking more hatred and desire for vengeance against us for killing their families or friends? It's past time to stop forcing our soldiers to fight and die for a metaphor.

It's past time our media refused to let Mr. Bush get away with phony one-liners.

MUSLIM-AMERICAN TURN-AROUND

On a college campus, an ambitious young reporter has come upon a Muslim student and decides to make a name for himself by doing a smashing interview.

Reporter: You are a Muslim?

Muslim: Yes, I am.

Reporter: And are you aware that Muslims perpetrated the attack on 9'11?

Muslim: Yes, I have so heard, and I regret that.

Reporter: Excellent! But you do know that many Muslims in the Middle East appear hostile to America and the western world?

Muslim: I have so heard.

Reporter: As a Christian myself, I feel aggrieved that such hostility has provoked attacks in London, Spain, Greece, Egypt and, uh, lots of other places, see. Are Muslims at all disturbed by such—let's say, unfriendly acts?

Muslim: Many of us are disturbed, indeed.

Reporter: Excellent! But tell me, why does your religion encourage such violence?

Muslim: Actually, my religion teaches love to all peoples, even to all animals.

Reporter: Mine too! But hey, Christians do not urge our faithful to attack people around the world where we may have some little differences, see what I mean?

Muslim: You do not?

Reporter: No way, Jose! I mean—Ibraham!

Muslim: But at present, are you not at war with a Muslim country, Iraq?

Reporter: Well, yeah, uh, but that's because we thought they had WMD—well, that didn't work, so, uh, to free that country from a terrible dictator, Saddam! Yeah! And our president has said often that what he wants is to bring peace to Iraq!

Muslim: Peace through war? How original! Could you tell me, do you know how many Iraqi citizens have been killed in that effort to bring "peace to Iraq"?

Reporter: Why, not exactly, but I can tell you how many American soldiers have been—

Muslim: More than 650,000 men, women and children have died. Bombing homes has crushed whole families to death—has this ever happened to you under an enemy attack?

Reporter: Ho boy, no! But we are afraid of another 9/11 attack, those violent Muslims, see.

Muslim: Yes, as many Middle East countries are afraid you will attack them, because they see so many of your warships, soldiers and planes all around them.

Reporter: But our soldiers are there to keep peace, remember?

Muslim: Of course—is that why you went to war with Vietnam too?

Reporter: Well, let's see now, yeah, and to keep Communism under control or something, see.

Muslim: I see. So you had to kill 3,200,000 people of that small land—tell me, in nine years, did you accomplish your purpose?

Reporter: Did we accomplish—hey, look, that was way before my time, see, but—

Muslim: Of course. And even before that, five years after World War II, when your President Roosevelt and Winston Churchill and General Eisenhower all said there must be no more wars, did not you wage war against North Korea, in which about a million people died?

Reporter: Yeah? They did? Hey, listen, like I said, I'm just a sophomore here, see, so—

Muslim: I understand, of course, but perhaps you recall how your friendly President Reagan invaded a tiny, peaceful little island and killed a few natives there and a few of your young soldiers too, and also secretly waged war through mercenaries against a struggling neighbor, Nicaragua, killing 36,000 innocent people there?

Reporter: Yeah? I never read anything about that in my history books—

Muslim: Of course, only a small war, little covered by your media. But do you remember your first President Bush—did he not invade a small country of Panama whose leader had been his buddy, killing natives and destroying homes, seizing that leader and taking him to your state of Florida where he was tried and imprisoned?

Reporter: Uh, well, that is a little unusual, isn't it, but—

Muslim: I would hazard a guess that if one of your presidents were kidnapped, you would not take it lightly. But then this same president, did he not form a coalition to rush into Iraq to stop Saddam from invading Kuwait, destroying the country's water purification and sewage plants so that impure water in the next ten years killed more than a million elderly, children and babies, most vulnerable to impure water?

Reporter: No kidding? I never heard about that—

Muslim: May I ask, have you heard about the use of depleted uranium in your nation's artillery that caused much harm in your own soldiers and has caused horribly deformed births in Iraqi women who—

Reporter: Hold on a minute—I've never heard about depleted uranium—you sure about that?

Muslim: Indeed, I learned about it on your TV program, 60 Minutes, and I have heard that it is being used today in Iraq.

Reporter: Well, I'll be darned if—

Muslim: But coming back closer to your present time, I'm sure you recall how your President Bush the Younger, angered over the attack of 9/11, charged into Afghanistan where the perpetrator, bin Laden, was said to be hiding, and your heavy bombing killed and wounded thousands of innocents.

Reporter Yeah, yeah, I guess so, but as you said, we were hunting down that evil guy, bin Laden, see.

Muslim: Ah, of course, and did you find him?

Reporter: C'mon, you know we didn't, cause we went into Iraq instead!

Muslim: And created chaos. But forgive me, I have taken too much of your time. Do you have any more questions for me?

Reporter: Yeah—how do I get outta here?

TURNING THE TABLES, SHOCKINGLY, FICTIONALLY

If terrorists from Canada had attacked a notable site in Italy, and Italy had retaliated against Canada by bombing heavily and taking out its government, and then because Italy did not like our president it began a costly war against OUR nation, how would we respond?

(I love Italy, its music, its art, its people; this is hypothetical, for making a point.)

What if the Italian army hit Washington so hard that our government was defeated, and they attempted to take over everything? They would claim that they were waging a "war on terrorism" to justify their killing of 100,000 innocent American citizens in their invasion, burning hundreds of children to death, in one bombing raid on a home in Cleveland killing six members of a man's family—his wife and five children. What if this father and husband stood grieving on our TV sets saying "I had to dig out their bodies with my bare hands—then I had to bury them with my bare hands!" Would we feel gratitude, patience—or rage and hatred toward the bombers?

What if a father in Chicago who had at first welcomed the new foreign power since he had disliked our president, but then said on a news program as he sat weeping in a hospital—"At first I thought things might be better for us laborers, but now my only son had his face blown off in your missile attack! Why did you do this? What did we ever do to you to make you do this to us? Nothing! Nothing!!" He sits beside his unconscious child in the hospital, weeping. How would we feel about this?

What if a father in Memphis lamented the loss from Italy's heavy bombing of NINE members of his family? How could this father go on living—and would he respect and cooperate with Italy in its planning of our new government, more like Italy's—a little socialism, more money on building up military might, national health care, the invader's decision to donate more money to what THEY liked, and other changes we were not familiar with or even disapproved?

What if nearby countries that shared much of our culture were incited by Italy's destructive invasion to join us in fighting? Would we welcome them? Would we appreciate their sharing of our sacrifices and casualties? What if the invaders were confronted with resistance by our patriotic citizens now enraged by the killing of so many of our innocent people who had done absolutely nothing harmful to Italy? What if the invaders kept up their bombing and forced entry into our homes, tearing up the rooms in search for weapons, pushing our citizens out of the way—in their own homes?

What if these invaders still hadn't given us back clean and safe water after having destroyed it in a previous war, and their sanctions of a dozen years had prevented the purification of our water so that a million of our children, babies and elderly, those most vulnerable to impure water, had died as a result? Would those fighting back against the Italian invaders-occupiers be insurgents, enemies, or patriotic citizens fighting to defend our country?

What if invader-Italy decreed that we would be allowed to have our own government modeled on its own by a certain date, but that Italy would take over a beautiful huge building for its own embassy with about 3,000 members watching over all of our activities, constructing 14 new military bases—in Dallas, in Pittsburgh, Orlando, Denver—without asking us if this was okay?

What if many nations in our hemisphere and in Europe had been strongly against Italy's invasion of our country, and the United Nations had been against the war, so that a great mass of hostility around the world was directed toward Italy? Would Italy be waging a war that would lessen terrorism against it—or increase it?

If Italy's president had said after that early terrorist attack on one of its landmarks that "there are terrorists in 68 nations," could Italy possibly invade 68 countries to find the terrorists and capture or kill them all? Wouldn't we be rising up against such a devastating power ourselves if Italy continued to use its superior military might on Buffalo and Sacramento and Boston, destroying historic sections of our cities, and daily taking lives of our men, women and children? If our hospitals were full of our children who had their legs or arms blown off? Horrible burns on their faces, perhaps lost their hands when picking up one of thousands of those cluster bombs that look like cute, colorful cans of something tasty?

What if Italy was still using depleted uranium in its artillery, which twelve years before had had such debilitating effects on its own soldiers and caused terrible abnormal births to our American mothers, short arms, no arms, huge heads, three arms? Would the people all around the world aware of this feel friendly to Italy, or resent its indifference to civilian wounds and deaths?

The Chinese have a well-known saying: "You can't know what a man is feeling unless you can walk in his shoes for 24 hours." At least we can try to imagine what people of other nations are feeling if we consider ourselves as victims of conquest, instead of the invader.

MEMORIES OF DISTANT WARS

Strange how our mind chooses what to think of, what to direct us to do, what it chooses to remember, what to forget. There are two images of war, our American wars that cling to my mind like cellophane, as if they are of family members, loved, enjoyed, and lost.

It was some time in the 1980's in the war President Ronald Reagan chose to inflict upon small, struggling Nicaragua, ever our neighbor to the south, ever an object of our commercial and military interest. When the people finally overthrew their brutal dictator, Anastasio Somoza, Reagan decided that he would not accept the new government of Daniel Ortega and the Sandinistas, who were liberating the peasants, eliminating polio, and expanding health care into rural areas where they had never seen a doctor or a nurse.

I belonged to a unique organization called Witness for Peace that kept track of the war Reagan delivered to the Nicaraguans through mercenaries, called Contra, from nearby countries such as Honduras. These volunteers could use the money we paid them, since that part of our Americas was poor, jobs scarce. Each week the reports told of attacks, where, damage done, how many peasants injured, how many killed. One week a bulletin described a story so deeply moving that I did not want to believe it, couldn't erase it from my mind, not ever:

One morning, a little five-year-old girl heard the doorbell ring, wondered if it was her aunt or grandmother, maybe a friend coming to play. She started to the door, but her father playfully decided to race her, see who could get to the door first. The two laughingly raced anxiously to the door, who would win—the daddy or the child?

When they pulled the door open, there stood about ten or 11 Contra, the enemy force dressed in uniforms my government had supplied them, holding guns my government had supplied them. They immediately shot the father, who fell dead to the floor, then they shot the little girl, who fell to the floor just inside the door . . . a child eager and innocent, lying in her red blood, her playful race ended in a moment by American bullets. Her father may have been a member of the Sandinista Party, so was slated to be killed. But why the child?

Then a mother of little girls myself, I could see in my mind's eye the terrified mother running to see what the shots were, desperately hoping her husband had not been killed—and the horror of seeing both her husband and her little child lying in streams of blood in her doorway, both lifeless! The fun of the father and daughter racing each other to the door, laughing and eager to see who would be at their door and who would win? Surely the daddy would have let his little girl win their race . . . and then the shock, the unbelievable nightmare of soldiers in my country's uniforms, holding my country's guns, unbelievably killing not only the father but this little girl whose smiling, eager face I see at unpredicted times, when reading about our latest war and deaths of children, children killed by our American bombs, our missiles, once again . . . I sometimes hear the mother's scream at the ghastly sight . . . the little girl running, running, laughing, eager . . . nameless, but alive in my memory . . . .

The cousin memory, sometimes the two together, is of an Iraqi father shown on CNN in a program detailing our Iraq Invasion . . . a tall man, lean, with mustache only, probably in his forties, standing beside a great heap of rubble on a street of rubble . . . "Look what you did, look what your bombs did!" he cried in a dazed and deadened voice. "I came home from a business trip and my house was this heap of rubble! My wife and my five little children were crushed to death by your bombs! I had to dig out their bodies with my bare hands! And then I had to bury them—with my bare hands! My wife of 24 years! Killed by your bombs! How can I go on living?"

He held up a photograph of a small girl, pretty and smiling. "This is my little girl, just five years old, she was so smart—now she is dead! All of my five children and my wife dead—from your terrible bombs!" He broke into tears. "What did we ever do to you that you would do this to us? Why? Why?"

Cheney-Bush-Rumsfeld-Wolfowitz have never answered.

These two memories cling to my mind like cellophane, two little girls, looking alike, dark hair, smiling, innocent . . . dead by my country's machinery of war . . . many wars, wars unending . . . .

THE WORLD WOULD BE
A BETTER PLACE

The world would be a better place
if people could purr and growl,
hiss and bark like our für favored pets.
Great feats of brilliant beneficence
solely for justice and generosity,
no personal profit, but progress
and peace for a welcoming world
would inspire a symphony of purring
and joyful yipping resounding
like a counterpoint to Mahler
or Rachmaninoff's Third Concerto,
glorious and gratifying for the princes
to hear, knowing their performance
was approved, appreciated by the populace.
But when a war explodes
for dominance and protected profit,
Dismissing death and devastation,.
Graft or corruption of cruel crafting,
The roar of barking and furious hissing
Rising in street and countryside
Would block all media and communication,
And holding their ears could not hold back
The fury of the people to their leaders.
So heartless princes, presidents,
vice presidents and all players
in the government's palaces
or Houses of White would recoil,
hide, and finally, to lower
the deafening roar and their fear,
alter the offensive acts, cancel the war,
bring soldiers home to love and live.
So would the world stir princes and presidents
To wiser, just and more gratifying intentions,
If only citizens could growl and hiss, purr and bark
Like our discerning dogs and cats, alas!

IMPRISON, HUMILIATE, TORTURE

I'm lucky. I live in a safe little New England town. I have never been in prison, never known anyone who has been, never been tortured. Any one of these three conditions must be a horror.

Horrors that my own country has been producing for five years. I've read reports of those who have been imprisoned, humiliated and tortured in my country's prisons—at Guantanamo, in Abu Ghraib, in other unidentified countries where torture is routine. During the first year, I assumed that someone was checking up on these tales, some members of Congress surely would be aware of these actions. For our Constitution states clearly that Congress "make Rules concerning Captures on Land and Water." Not the president, not our military, not the vice-president.

Even now, in late 2007, it seems that about a thousand or more men are living in inhuman conditions, shackled, arms chained to the ceiling, stuck in solitary confinement, and most incredible of all—with no charge against them! Our president enjoys his mantra about "Freedom and Liberty," but he—the ultimate power—has been depriving fellow human beings of "Freedom and Liberty."

I'm lucky. I've always had family to turn to when I needed help at any time—so it's difficult to imagine being trapped a thousand or more miles away from my home in, say, a Muslim culture, in some kind of prison where no one spoke my language. I could not tell anyone if I felt weak or sick or dizzy, or just in panic because I did not know where I was, who were the people around me, and why was this happening?

The Chinese have a saying—"You never know how another person is feeling unless you can walk in his shoes for 24 hours." It would be valuable for President Bush or Vice President Cheney to be swept away from Washington by a strange hooded figure, blindfolded and stashed away in the trunk of a car, let out to be hooded and shoved into what sounds like a plane being warmed up for flight—where were we going?! What terror! To be taken away somewhere by strangers—why? Who were these people speaking a strange language? What was going to happen to me, George Bush, me, Dick Cheney!

Can we ourselves imagine this happening to us? Is this possible in our country? In a far country, maybe? Then, day after day imagine wondering "Where am I, what torture will come next, where is my family, are they all right, will they come to save me? Why are my hands attached to those hard chains to the ceiling? How long can I stand like this, hour after hour, and not die! Imagine counting the days and nights—20, 50, 100, 365, 450, losing count after 500 days, sleeping and praying, sleeping and praying for help, for freedom, for someone who seems human and will talk to me in my own language and explain this horror to me . . . and offer me help! Help! HELP ME!!

A needless war, loss of soldiers all young and hopeful, or brutally wounded, Post Traumatic Stress Disorder for years or for life—plus the killing of thousands of innocents—now reaching a million human lives—in another country who had done us no harm. War is barbaric. But if we take the barbaric step into a war, at least we must not toss aside our own rules of warfare. The concerned mantra is—"Do we want our soldiers to be treated in this way?" This is asked by Sen. John McCain, held and tortured in the Vietnam War.

Then we must treat those we capture, for insubstantial reasons, fairly, in accordance with rules of the Geneva Conventions and our own Constitution. But we know that in this war thousands have been seized and imprisoned without charges. Picking up a man who looks like a Muslim in a New York City airport, sweeping him with no explanation over to a far country such as Syria for imprisonment and torture is a violation of our own laws, Constitution and human rights all over the world.

But it has been happening, is happening. Only in July of 2007 did President Bush finally declare that torture is banned from our detention centers—but is it? Imprisonment without charges, without legal help, without human restraint—in MY country? BY my country? Waterboading that our new Attorney General isn't sure is torture? Should he try it to learn if it is or not? How have we twisted so far from decency and human feeling?

Such terrorist actions should never have been taken by our leaders—by Donald Runmsfeld, Dick Cheney and their President, George Bush. Personally claiming himself a religious man, Mr. Bush should recall "Thou Shalt Not Kill," and "Do Unto Others as you would have done unto you."

Only Congress can demand an end to such inhuman conditions, our Constitution so decrees.

MOTHER AND CHILD
SPEAK OF WAR

Child: Mother, what is war?

Mother: War is an organized method of killing and destroying, child.

Child: But why would anyone want to do that?

Mother: Many reasons, apparently. Sometimes a country has a neighbor that is hurting them, or threatening some harsh action. So they attack them to prevent this from happening.

Child: I see, and do we have such neighbors near US, Mother?

Mother: No, child, we have friendly neighbors above and below us, and beautiful oceans on each side.

Child: Then we do not have to have any wars, do we, Mother?

Mother: In a way that is true, my child, but we still have many wars, more than almost any other country.

Child: We do? Why is that?

Mother: Many of our presidents have found reasons for war.

Child: What reasons could they have?

Mother: Difficult to say, my child. Sometimes they wanted to change a nation's form of government, sometimes they may have desired something the other country had or—

Child: But Mother, you said war is a way of killing—how do they do this?

Mother: I am afraid they make strong weapons of killing and wounding, very expensive bombs and missiles and guns, and planes that carry these things to—

Child: Mother, I cannot believe you! In school we are taught to settle our problems in a friendly way, never to hit or hurt anyone!

Mother: Ah, that is the right way, my child. I wish that your school was in charge of our government's relations with the rest of the world and—

Child: But Mother, this cannot be true! I do not want to believe my country would do such things, no, no!

Mother: Oh, my dear child, I am sorry—come here! You are crying—we should all be crying!

QUOTES ABOUT WAR BY WISE MEN

Our nation began this brand new century with two wars.

Many of our country's presidents—Roosevelt, Eisenhower, John Kennedy, and Lincoln—have spoken forcefully against war. European nations, having lived through the Second World War on their soil, have formed the European Union to settle problems peacefully. Now, as we are engaged in our eighth war since World War II, it might be worthwhile to reflect on thoughts on war from great leaders through the centuries:

WWII General, Republican President Dwight Eisenhower: I hate war, as only a soldier who has been there can, who has seen its brutality, its futility, its stupidity!

I like to believe that our people are going to do more to promote peace than our governments. Indeed, I think that people want peace so much that one of these days governments had better get out of the way and let them have it!

Benjamin Franklin: There never was a bad peace or a good war.

Cicero: Laws are silent in time of war.

President John F. Kennedy: Mankind must put an end to war, or war will put an end to mankind. War will exist until that distant day when the conscientious objector enjoys the same reputation and prestige that the warrior does today.

Herodotus: In peace, sons bury their fathers, but war violates the order of nature, and fathers bury sons.

President Franklin D. Roosevelt: More than an end to war, we want an end to the beginning of all wars—yes, an end to this brutal, inhuman and thoroughly impractical method of settling the differences between governments!

Abraham Lincoln: The best way to destroy an enemy is to make him a friend.

Martin Luther King Jr.: Love is the only force capable of turning an enemy into a friend.

Dr. King: Our scientific power has outrun our spiritual power. We have guided missiles and misguided men.

The Bible: Blessed are the Peacemakers, for they shall inherit the earth.

The Bible, the Beatitude: Thou Shalt Not Kill!

Erasmus: The most disadvantageous peace is better than the most just war.

George Bush: We're bringing peace to Iraq, peace to the Middle East!
Confucius: We can't use war as an instrument to bring peace.

Ralph Bunche, early chairman of the United Nations: There are no warlike people, just warlike leaders.

President Eisenhower: Beware the military-industrial complex!

Muriel Lester, British pacifist and labor leader: War is as outmoded as cannibalism, chattel slavery, blood feuds and dueling, an insult to God and humanity, a daily crucifixion of Christ.

Mohandas Gandhi: I object to violence because when it appears to do good, the good is only temporary; the evil it does is permanent.

George Bernard Shaw: Peace is not only better than war, but infinitely more arduous.

John Courtney Murray, Jesuit priest and editor: There is never a time when citizens should be more vocal in their criticism than when their government is killing people in their name.

John Lennon: All we are saying is, Give peace a chance!

Martin Luther King: Our nation is the greatest purveyor of violence in the world.
Dr. King: If humanity is to progress, Gandhi is inescapable; he lived, thought and acted inspired by the vision of humanity evolving toward a world of peace and harmony. We may ignore him at our own risk.

President Eisenhower: Every gun that's made, every warship launched, every rocket fired signifies, in the final sense, a theft from those who hunger and are not fed, those that are cold and are not clothed. The world in arms is not spending alone. It is spending the sweat of laborers, the genius of its scientists, the hopes of its children. This is not a way of life at all, in any true sense. Under the cloud of threatening war, it is humanity hanging from an iron cross!

THE NEW MATH—MORE OF US KILLED BY GUNS THAN BY WARS?

Math has never been my strong point. But some numbers impress me, even stun me:

Deaths in attack on New York's World Trade Towers on 9/11: **3,000**
Deaths of our soldiers in Iraq in the last four years: **3,719**
U.S. soldiers wounded, maimed, disabled in the Iraq War: **24,912**
U.S. citizens killed by guns in the last four years: **121,000**

We're all lucky if we haven't lost someone we love in one of our many wars—8 since World War II.

We're all lucky if we haven't lost someone we love who was struck dead by a gun.

Citizens in most European nations haven't lost anyone they love in either of these kinds of violence since the end of World War II. The European Union was formed after World War II to avoid wars by settling problems diplomatically—as urged by Britain's Winston Churchill and our President Roosevelt at that war's end. Britain joined us in our ill-chosen Iraq War, and a few other nations sent small contingencies of soldiers.

There is another side to our eight wars since WW II, of course, the side we took to war:

Vietnamese killed in the Vietnam War, 1963-1975: **3,200,000**
U.S. soldiers lost in Vietnam: **58,178**
Iraqis killed by our invasion: **100,000**
Total of Iraqi deaths by our invasion plus their civil war: **755.000**
Estimates of Iraqi deaths, late 2007: **1,000,000**

When facing these figures, Americans sometimes ask—why are we so violent?

Looking over these figures, a person could conclude that we Americans don't care as much about human life as the rest of the world, which suffers so much less from violence; except in revolutionary places like Darfur. Yet in many ways we get along with each other better than disparate groups in many other countries; we are on record as being one of the most religious countries on earth, and we have no large conflicts between our many different faiths. Our religions respect human life. When the Iraq War was threatened, vast numbers of citizens marched in protest all over the world and Catholic bishops, Methodist bishops, clergy of almost all of our faiths spoke out in fervent opposition.

For some much-questioned reason, President Bush and Vice-President Cheney had planned this war since they were elected in 2000, according to then Secretary of the Treasury Paul O'Neill who cited especially Cheney, Defense Secretary Rumsfeld and Paul Wolfowitz as those most anxious for attacking Iraq. These men were founding members of the Project for a New American Century, which had asked President Clinton to invade Iraq and take out Saddam in 1998.

For the first three years, Americans for the most part supported the war, our traditional patriotism directing us once more to back up our troops. But now in our fourth year of heavy losses, and no end in sight with eruption of the Iraq civil war, most Americans are discouraged, angry, and asking hard questions—when is the end? How many more tours of duty for our war-weary soldiers? When are we pulling out?

And then, the shocking shooting of 32 students and teachers at Virginia Tech. More shock, more violence, more deaths, more lack of control, lack of security, in contrast to the President's constant message of how he is "protecting my people!" Where was security for the innocents on that lovely campus?

General and Republican President Eisenhower seriously warned us about the dangers of the Military Industrial Complex. Recent reports state that our nation is the Number One purveyor of military arms in the world, extending the dangerous power of our weaponry

Arc the gun makers aligned with the powerful military suppliers? Our National Rifle Association is a strong lobbyist. In other countries around the world, similar companies have not held enough power to prevent gun controls that allow low figures on homicide by guns. Why such a problem here? Many Congressmen have tried to pass laws limiting gun access, but have never gotten enough support. Senator Kennedy, who lost brothers John and Bobby to gunfire, hoped to pass legislation to limit the availability of handguns. The late Senator John Chafee of Rhode Island tried for years to achieve protective legislation for our people—but finally gave up.

So every year, our nation shocks the world by experiencing about 30,000 deaths by guns, especially prevalent in our big city areas of poor citizens lacking power. In European cities if a person wants to purchase a gun, he must first apply for a license at a police station. This may take a couple of months, or even a couple of years; then he may buy only a rifle for hunting—no handguns. A few countries that did experience severe shooting incidents among children, such as Scotland and Australia, soon passed strict gun laws preventing further tragedies. Why have we not?

Many gun owners point to the assurance given them by our Second Amendment; this famous document was created during the beginning of our country, when no national army existed; thus that new government wanted states to have their own militias.

In cases before our Supreme Court, the judges have so declared. Here a quote from the renowned Warren E. Burger, former Chief Justice of the U.S. Supreme Court:

"Few things have been more vigorously debated—and distorted—in recent tines as the meaning of the Second Amendment . . . The real purpose of the Second Amendment was to ensure that "state armies'—'the militia'—would be maintained "for the defense of the state."

"The very language of the Second Amendment refutes any argument that it was intended to guarantee any citizen an unfettered right to any kind of weapon he or she desires." (11/26/1991)

Other cases before the Supreme Court and lesser courts have resulted in similar decisions, such as "United States vs. Warin, in 1992. Convicted of owning a machine gun, Warin claimed that his right to own a "true military weapon" was protected by the Second Amendment. However, the 8th Circuit Court maintained that "With the passage of the Dick Act in 1903, the states militias were organized into the National Guard structure, which remains in place today. Considering this history, we cannot conclude that the Second Amendment protects individual possession of military weapons."

In 1996. an aspiring bodyguard sought a concealed weapons right in both Los Angeles and San Francisco, but found his application denied. He then filed suit against these cities, saying that they had denied his Second Amendment rights. However, his appeal to Second Amendment rights was denied by the

Ninth Court, which ruled that the "Second Amendment protected only a state's right to keep and maintain an armed militia."

Similarly, in the case of Morton Grove, Illinois, which banned the sale and possession of handguns in 1982, gun owners objected, claiming violation of their Second Amendment rights. But the U. S. Seventh Court disagreed, stating that "the right to keep and bear handguns is not guaranteed by the Second Amendment." The Supreme Court refused to review the case, showing its agreement with the decision of the lower court.

No other country suffers such terrible losses of their citizens' lives—more than 30,000 deaths by guns each year. No other country wages so many wars as we do—8 since WWII, with losses of hundreds of thousands of American lives, not to dismiss the millions of lives in nations we attack, provoking resentment toward us that can lead to desire for vengeance through terrorist acts.

We have, once again, a change of government, Democrats in control—well, mostly in control. Will they ignore such massive losses to human life? When they see the grieving parents of life-loving young students killed at Virginia Tech, and the grieving parents of life-loving young soldiers killed in a needless war in Iraq, will they do nothing?

QUOTES ON WAR:

President Eisenhower,
Author, Professor Andrew Bacevich

GENERAL AND PRESIDENT EISENHOWER SAID:
'EVERY GUN THAT'S MADE, EVERY WARSHIP LAUNCHED, EVERY ROCKET FIRED SIGNIFIES, IN THE FINAL SENSE, A THEFT FROM THOSE WHO HUNGER AND ARE NOT FED, THOSE WHO ARE COLD AND ARE NOT CLOTHED. THE WORLD IN ARMS IS NOT SPENDING ALONE, IT IS SPENDING THE SWEAT OF ITS LABORERS, THE GENIUS OF ITS SCIENTISTS, THE HOPES OF ITS CHILDREN . . . THIS IS NOT A WAY OF LIFE AT ALL, IN ANY TRUE SENSE. UNDER THE CLOUD OF THREATENING WAR, IT IS HUMANITY HANGING FROM AN IRON CROSS!

ANDREW BACEVICH, AUTHOR 'THE NEW AMERICAN MILITARISM,' WRITES:
'TODAY, AS NEVER BEFORE IN THEIR HISTORY, AMERICANS ARE ENTHRALLED WITH MILITARY POWER. LIBERALS AND CONSERVATIVES ALIKE HAVE REACHED A COMMON UNDERSDTANDING THAT SCATTERING U.S. TROOPS AROUND THE GLOBE TO RESTRAIN, INFLUENCE, PERSUADE OR CAJOLE PAYS DIVIDENDS.

WHETHER ANY CORRELATION EXISTS BETWEEN THIS VAST PANOPLY OF DEPLOYED FORCES AND ANTIPATHY TO THE UNITED STATES IS A TABOO SUBJECT. THE NEW AMERICAN MILITARISM MANIFESTS ITSELF THROUGH AN INCREASED PRPOPENSITY TO USE FORCE, LEADING, IN EFFECT, TO THE NORMALIZATION OF WAR. "

EARLY IN THE MILITARY HIMSELF, BACEVICH HAS GROWN TO DEEP CONCERN ABOUT OUR MILITARY'S ACTIONS. IN JUNE, 2007, HIS SON WAS KILLED IN IRAQ.

GEORGE BUSH HAS CONSTANLY SAID ALL DURING THE IRAQ WAR:
"WE'RE BRINGING PEACE TO IRAQ, WE'RE BRINGING PEACE TO THE MIDDLE EAST" . . . BUT CONFUCIUS SAID: "WE CANNOT USE WAR AS AN UINSTRUMNENT TO BRING PEACE . . ."

WE NEVER APOLOGIZE

A few years back, a popular novel by Eric Segal titled "Love Story" had a much-quoted line made even more popular in the movie version as delivered by actress Ali McGraw: "Love means never having to say you're sorry."

I never thought much of that line, it sounded a bit corny. I think you should always apologize when you do something that hurts someone, or a group of persons. But it seems that our government leaders took to the line, even before Eric Segal wrote it. Because as a nation, we never apologize for any wrong or harm we do to people—our own citizens or human beings in other nations. We don't even, as a visible nation, ever admit to wrongdoing, nor appear to feel any regret or sympathy toward those we have hurt severely.

The grammar school bully, who steals a girl's hat, pushes a more timid boy down stairs—this bully is disliked as well as feared by his classmates. A responsible principal will take this boy aside and try to make him understand how cowardly his actions are, how they make so many students and even faculty dislike him. He would try to make the tough kid understand that cooperation and helpfulness make more friends than hanging tough.

The principal might compel this troublesome boy to apologize to the girl whose hat he stole and to the boy he knocked down the stairs, helping the rambunctious kid to learn how to say he's sorry—how to really FEEL sorry. If he continues offensive acts, his parents may be called in with possibility of his being expelled.

Our trouble is that there is no "responsible principal" available to tell Uncle Sam that he has been a bully long enough, time to stop hurting and killing innocent people, sending our troops into small countries like Panama and Nicaragua to hold power over their people, or placing by force a leader subservient to us and indifferent to the needs of his own citizens.

The nations of the Middle East, with obvious reasons, fear our attack. Countries in Europe fear our attack. According to the report read to Jon Stewart of the Daily Show by Madeleine Albright, even China and Russia fear we might attack them! Are we proud to be the source of such fear? Apparently some of us are like the eighth grade bully who loves being the toughest guy who can beat up every other kid in school.

Without a responsible principal we will listen to, we are the world's bully who has just killed more than 100,000 innocent Iraqis, and more than 3,800 of our own very young soldiers, accomplished easily with our arsenal of the most powerful, ghastly, lethal weapons the world has ever seen. Like the school bully's stash of snowballs or rocks to toss at kids, we keep building up this supply, more, more, more though the cost is so great it makes us neglect matters of health, environment, education, safety—the bullies are apparently in charge our nation's "school," and no principal is in sight. Where can the wounded and harmed and resentful go?

To the United Nations, perhaps . . . yes, but the U.N. protested our war in Iraq, but our tough guys in control didn't even notice. When Ronald Reagan was president in the 1980's, the U.N. protested our war by mercenaries in Nicaragua—but Reagan paid no attention, and few leaders in Congress were perturbed enough to protest forcefully. If they did, the media continued to ignore our destructive action in our poor and struggling little neighbor.

We've had a lot of influence in that little neighbor. Early in the last century we kept watch over its land and harbors. A young activist named Sandino tried unsuccessfully to get our Marines and our influence out of his country. He was killed somehow instead. For many years our nation worked congenially with the cruel dictator Anastasio Somoza. Our president Roosevelt, too, maintained cooperative relations with him. "He's an s.o.b.," admitted Roosevelt, "but he's OUR s.o.b.!"

Our United Fruit Company did a fine business there, working nicely with Somoza to rule the country. Finally, in 1978 the people rose up to at last get rid of Somoza and bring freedom and rights to the Nicaraguan people. Did we help them. as we assert we invaded Iraq to get rid of the vicious dictator Saddam? No, we tried to help Somoza, and when the revolutionaries, called Sandinistas after the earlier leader Sandino, finally ousted him, our President Reagan began a subtle campaign to turn their revolution around. He ordered our military to find, arm and pay mercenaries from nearby states, such as Honduras, to bomb and kill Nicaraguans, destroy bridges, attack clinics that had in a year's time eliminated polio and almost eliminated malaria, in a vicious attempt to end the people's own revolution to oust a Saddam-like dictator.

During this troubling time, a young American engineer named Ben Linder went to Nicaragua to help the impoverished people find needed springs for water. He was a popular hero to the natives because he was also a clown, riding a unicycle and doing tricks for the children, and adults too. One day he was squatting with a Nicaraguan at a cite he discerned was promising for water—but a Contra, a man from a neighboring country whom we armed and clothed, came up close to him and shot him in the head, killing him.

The Sandinistas were socially progressive, perhaps Socialist-like, though not Communist. Their goal was to provide equality for their citizens, let them share the wealth of their country. But Reagan, coming to power in 1980, was determined to vilify their leader, Daniel Ortega, constantly referring him as "That dirty little Commie dictator in designer jeans."

Finally, after almost eight years of our attacks on their people and infrastructure, the rebels had to give in. Time then for an election to take place—so a group of AMERICANS was sent there to plan their election. Our problem in attaining a government that would be friendly to our corporations was that the most popular party was the Sandinistas. We couldn't let them win fairly, so OUR organizers set up a coalition of all of the other parties—11 of them from right wing to left (talk about principles!). Little noted in our press was the fact that on the left of the coalition was the REAL Communist Party which we paid to join our friendly coalition!

Reagan's name-calling had been false. He wasn't embarrassed by this, because little attention was paid to the election by any of our media.

What was the cost of our interference in that beleaguered country? First of all, they had lost 40,000 fighters in their revolution. Then our Contra forces killed 36,000 innocent civilians. In one episode I cannot forget, a five-year-old girl was running to see who was at the door, a playmate maybe, a grandmother or aunt? Her father joined her in seeing who could run faster . . . when they opened the door, there stood about a dozen Contra in U.S. supplied uniforms, holding U.S. guns—first they shot the father, then shot and killed the little girl. American mothers can imagine the horror of that mother.

Since our invasion by mercenaries, the gains in sharing its wealth, in providing rights for its people that they fought so valiantly for in their revolution have gone awry, their poverty and struggles all returned.

We have never apologized for our interference in their revolution, in their hopes for the freedom for which we Americans fought in our own revolution. Our government leaders have never learned the words, "We're sorry." Who can hope that Mr. Bush-Cheney-Runsfeld-Wolfowitz-Libby will one day say to the Iraqi people, "Please forgive us for killing 100,000 of your innocent people, and destroying so much of your land . . . we're really sorry . . ." Not a shudder of guilt is observed in our Republican leaders, in those Democrats who, now strongly critical, voted for this war.

We never say "We're sorry . . ."

FACING THE TRUTH—A STICKY WICKET FOR CHILDREN, PRESIDENTS AND CONGRESS

It's often hard to face the truth. Psychologists knew this. Many ministers and priests know this. Some teachers know this—not easy to tell a proud mother that her son isn't the top student in class, and even has some learning problems.

Some husbands and wives resist the truth—they'd rather keep hoping that things will get better and divorce won't be necessary

Recognizing the truth is a start for improving a relationship, a job, a leaky cellar. This same struggle to see the truth is a problem for our president. His cocky manner, litany of progress in Iraq, and adamant refusal to listen to different views from Congressional leaders show that he cannot face the truth.

Often the stumbling block is that admitting the truth will reflect badly on you. This is why a small child will lie about grabbing someone else's cookie. In some cases, with children or with criminals, facing the truth means punishment. For some people, even admitting a minor fault is not easy—a wife not wanting a tell her husband that dinner was late because she spent hours talking on the phone, so she makes a better excuse.

Oh well, no lives lost. But with our president, lives ARE lost, have been lost; will be lost because he has refused to face the truth. Lying about weapons of mass destruction and nuclear (nuculer) advances were bad enough—they might have been forgiven if he had not based the horror of war on them. When he had to admit the truth about these matters, he should have apologized—instead of hanging tough and substituting other less substantive, phony reasons for waging a war.

In situations of lying, a lot depends on second parties—a teacher who sees the pupil's lie and lets it go is at fault.

Similarly, for several years the majority of our population was forgiving, even backed the president's war while knowing it was based on those lies. Well, a clever kid, after he admits his lie, night make up a good excuse—the boy whose cookie he took had stolen from him the day before. Oh well, a Mom can be a little forgiving. Maybe. But if she is honest, she will watch to make sure that her child realizes the value of being honest. Who could say that honesty isn't the best policy?

Vice-President Cheney perhaps? We have to wonder because of his unquestionable calm as he spoke about the meeting of Osama with an emissary of Saddam, also the never-wincing straight face he maintained as he spoke of Iraq's growing nuclear power with tubes from Niger. The same straight face he presented in 1994—brought back in focus in the summer of 2007—when declaring that it would be "a mistake" to try to take over Iraq because of the difficult factions there, actually using the word often used to describe Iraq today—it would be a "quagmire!" A stunning image of shifting convictions, shifting moralities. Here was a man with years of experience in international relations, side by side with a much less experienced man with bravura and popular appeal. A heady combination—and dangerous!

There is another truth that, incredibly, is being ignored by Congress and a wide swath of our population: Muslims are horrified and furious at our war against them, people who had nothing to do with 9/11—both President Bush and then Secretary Rumsfeld stated this truth on TV. We have now alienated a billion members of a religion we know little about—and our president and vice-president still don't sense that their killing of hundreds of thousands of Muslims, destroying their homes and infrastructure, is increasing hatred and desire for pay-back throughout the Middle East.

Our outrage at deaths of 3,000 Americans on 9/11 catapulted us into attacks in Afghanistan where the perpetrator, Osama, was in hiding. Although we did not find him, we killed about 1600 Afghans—13000 more human beings than killed on 9/Il, and wounded many more. If we did this because of our anger at deaths of 3000 Americans, what do we expect Muslims to do in retaliation for our killing more than 200,000 innocent Iraqi Muslims? Thousands more from the civil war we set the stage for? Tit for tat can be a risky game among nations. During the First Gulf War of Bush No. One, Iraq's water purification and sewage disposal plants were destroyed. As children and the elderly, most vulnerable to impure water, began to weaken and die, citizens from our country traveled there to help restore clean water. But they were frustrated by our sanctions that disallowed not only chlorine but also essential plumbing parts to be imported. About a million children died, and at least a half million elderly also.

Osama bin Laden has informed us of the reasons for his attack on 9/11: those "sanctions on Iraq" forbidding import of chlorine to purify their water—"One million Iraqi children have thus far died although they did nothing wrong." American policies toward Israel holding his wrath "until Peace reigns in Palestine." And the presence of our soldiers in the "holy land of Muhammad," Saudi Arabia, mostly now withdrawn.

It's painful to face the truth of such harmful actions that our government caused, along with Britain under Tony Blair. But can we avoid facing these truths if we want to protect our people from further attacks? Mr. Bush frequently says that "security for my people" is his top priority,

With losses of our very young American soldiers now more than 3800, how can the President not see the truth? Is it his pride—his father had two wars and maintained honor and fame, so how can he go down in defeat and dishonor? Is it the force of his vice-president that compels him to push the truth and soldiers' casualties aside?

Or is it the compliant Congress that since March of 2003 has allowed him to ignore the truth and accomplish the mission—war with Iraq—that Cheney, Wolfowitz, Libby and Feith all had wanted since 1998 but Clinton denied them? Why did only a minority in Congress see the truth in Bush-Cheney's. plans to invade Iraq? Why did Congress allow the needless war to keep going till Iraq reached a disastrous and unsolvable Civil War?

Seeing the truth of this tragic waste of human lives and our nation's reputation, what is holding Congress back from impeaching both President Bush and Vice-President Cheney? Will it overlook this president's crimes as another Congress overlooked Lyndon Johnson's Vietnam War that lasted more than nine years, took 58,000 American lives and 3,200,000 Vietnamese? Can't Congress see the truth in our military adventurism? Can any of them see the truth of the money being made in Iraq each day by the Military Industrial Complex and its friends the Contractors?

Will reporters continue to laugh at Bush's little jokes and not press him for truth? And will the world's Muslims resent and hate us more than ever because we continue a war against them, noticing clearly that our government—Congress—does not care enough about the deaths and chaos we have caused them to stop our president's power by impeachment? By cutting the funds for more weapons that kill Muslims?

Power corrupts. Most of us have seen the truth of this statement.

A POEM AFTER WAR
THAT CHILD, A WORLD AWAY

That child, that small child
Is far away, a world away;
That child in pain
Across oceans, far from me,
The child is in shock
In a land unknown to me;
The child has lost his legs,
That child so many miles from me;
That boy has only half his arms,
He's screaming in horror and pain!
But I cannot hear his cries,
Cannot see his anguished face
I am so far away, a world away,
In a safe and peaceful place.

How did this happen,
This terrible thing,
So many calm miles away?
Our President's war, his brilliant bombs
Tore off the boy's arms, his legs
On one of the war's quietest days.
He will never run with other boys
Or catch a ball at play,
Nor write a story, paint a picture—
And how will he eat his meals?

I do not know this little boy
Whose arms and legs were ripped off,
Torn easily by our smartest bombs
In a war my president wanted,
In a war his vice-president wanted,
In a land a world away,
In a land a world away.

COLIN POWELL REFLECTS AND PRAYS: FROM MY PLAY, "GOD TALKS TO GEORGE BUSH"

Colin Powell: Well, Lord, I guess this is it . . . Cheney, Rumsfeld, Wolfowitz for sure, they want this war, and Bush has been too busy to even see me . . . I don't think I have a chance anyway, the ships of war are on their way . . . Oh God, the soldier—how many this time? . . . I can see them . . . scared to death, but running forward, with fear, fear and courage! God, I wish you wouldn't let this happen again!

I've been praying, every day, Lord, asking what I should do . . . can I do anything? Is war going to help, somehow, somewhere? Can I do anything to get it all over with . . . with what? As little horror as possible? Too late now, Lord, too late to change my career—I am a soldier, a long time soldier, how could I change now, be a doctor and save lives? Too late . . . I go to the United Nations tomorrow, present my . . . evidence, some serious evidence . . . and hope it's true . . . I guess that's all I can do, Lord, now that I'm in this high position . . .

Yes, I wanted it, an advance for my people, but what for me . . . now? Another war, thousands of deaths, I can see the wounded now in their beds without arms, legs! Oh God! What am I getting into—again!

Lord, please help me get through this . . . with strength, with honor—honor? What does "honor" mean really? Doctors try to save lives . . . soldiers steal them from the young and innocent, on both sides . . .

Lord, help me, in your wisdom, be a guide, strength . . . Amen.

PART 2
SATIRES

GEORGE BUSH SPEAKS OUT ON FREEDOM AND LIBERTY

Listen, we got freedom and liberty, who can beat these fine things for takin' over the world, huh? Our enemies, listen, they got dark ideals, dark things, I don't want even ta think about them! And they hate our freedom, but listen, I'm not gonna give it up, not one half inch of it, nosiree, it's my God-given right to have that freedom even if nobody else in this nation of mine has as much of it as I do—I love that freedom—some men get up for that mornin' shot of java—me, I go for that full glass of freedom!

Freedom and liberty, we got FREEDOM to barge into any old Muslim country that happens to have weapons of mass destruction, we know they did—don't try to fool us, we know they did 'cause we helped 'em develop them! And we got liberty too, so we can take the LIBERTY of charging into a Muslim country and kill a coupla hundred thousand innocent Muslims if we feel like it, let them know who's the boss, see, and my Congress lets me do it! And we have the LIBERTY ta go after their oil 'cause Cheney and Wolfie and Rummy knew what's best for their oil—I mean for ALL their people, see, my people too, even though some a them are pushin' my ratings down a little here and there, as far as I read in the papers and I don't read much of those scandal sheets like the New York Tines, I get alla the important stuff from my great vice president, only I call him "Shooter" now, see, he gets a big kick outa that, almost makes him smile!

Yessirree, freedom and liberty! We're tryin' ta sell them to the whole Middle East, see, like that pesky little Hezbollah, they don't know what the words even mean, givin' hell to little Israel our best friend over there in that crazy part of the world, but they're learnin' 'cause we have the FREEDOM to hand over missiles and bombs to Israel, see, I'm takin' the LIBERTY of sendin' Condi over there even if she can't do anything except sound smart and play the piano—she sure plays a mean piano, though she's still workin' on some a those great Texas cowboy songs I like ta listen to—Beethoven and Mozart never had a chance to see the heart of Texas or they coulda probably turned out more manly kinda music.

Y'see, Israel has freedom like ours too, we more or less showed them how ta grow freedom and liberty, so they're tryin' ta show their neighbors those fine qualities too, but that dang Hezbollah doesn't seem grateful, so Israel took the LIBERTY of provin' just like us that they have the FREEDOM to throw bombs at Lebanon, maybe killin' a lotta babies and children, sure, but just like us in Iraq, they mean to do good and get Lebanon off their hind legs and toss out Hezbollah, then they might stop their bombin', see. And I admit that Israel looks up ta us as their friend and savior sorta, see, and if we're occupyin' Iraq they're gonna occupy Palestine, but they wanta bring freedom and liberty to Palestine too, just like I'm bnringin' freedom and liberty to Iraq, even if I have to stuff it down their Sunni and Shi'ia throats!

Some a my people feel they have a little less freedom and liberty these days, well, that's only temporary, see, till I get Iraq and Afghanistan and Lebanon and Hezbollah and Palestine and Iran and Syria all fixed up with my kind of FREEDOM and LIBERTY!

So juss wait a bit, my fellow Americans, my polls will be goin' up again, 'cause Dickie-boy and me are bringin' American style freedom to the whole dangerous Middle East, and sooner or later, those that live through it are gonna appreciate it. And lemme tell ya, any day now I'm gonna bring our great American FREEDOM and LIBEERTY back to alla you fine Americans too! Meanwhile, my people should appreciate that we got 14 great new bases in Iraq now, Shooter says we were runnin' short—we had only 679 big and little bases there in the Middle East before our invasion. Doesn't that warm the cockles of your patriotic American hearts? Lemme tell ya, when I just mention this ta my fine vice president, he almost smiles! I count a lot on Shooter, 'cause he really knows what our foreign policy is oil about!

Just like our Pledge of Allegiance says, "with Liberty and Justice for all"—any day now!

WHY NOT BOMB THEM—
RIGHT NOW!

Sure, let's bomb Iran! Why not? We got lots of bombs—smart, dumb, all kinds. Little and big nukes too!

They think they're so smart raking up a little nuculer power. Have they forgotten that we have a THOUSAND big ones? Listen, we drop a few of those big fellows on them, they'll know better than to make fun of our orders the next time!

It'll be a lesson for other smarties in the neighborhood too—hey, while we're at it, why not toss a few over Hezbollah in Lebanon? They never listen to us like most of their neighbors. And why not Syria? No kind words for our little spat in Iraq. Sure, we sent a few of those detainees over there for detention and torture, like that Canadian guy. But hey, who knew they'd torture the guy? Not us! Speaking of that little spat, can we forget that France has been really snippy to us, never a word of encouragement, never even a few croissants sent over to our brave fighting men and jeune fillles? Why not a couple of big ones on France, they think they're so superior! Maybe they wouldn't be so uppity if we reminded them who's the boss of this world, n'est pas?

Sure, some sourpusses will complain, "Hey, we're gonna make more enemies, more Muslims will hate us and maybe try a little terror stuff on us! Let's take it easy!" Easy? That's not our middle name—our middle name is "BOMBS AWAY!" While we're at it, North Korea has been a pain in the butt—that little country's chief thinks we won't drop a nuculer one on them 'cause maybe they got a nuculer one to toss at us? Well, we got news for you, buddy—just you try to sail a big one all the way to our shores! Ha! Not a chance, baby! Not a chance! But we got military hardware all around the Middle East, it wouldn't be a big deal for us at all! So watch it!

Speaking of distance, let's not forget that our neighbor Canada has been pretty snotty about our latest war, too, alla those marches and protests and dirty little digs n their media—I say let them have it! Teach them a lesson about how to be a Good Neighbor! Just think how nice a big one would look over Niagara Falls! The Canadian side!

Okay, so let's not forget South America, we've been real easy on them lately, ever since Nicaragua, Chile, El Salvador, Guatemala, Panama and alla those dinky little playlands—it's time we reminded them of who's the boss of this here hemisphere! Like that tough little show-off guy, Chavez in Venezuela—get him sendin' cheap oil to some of our poor people—what a nerve! Tryin' to make us look like pikers! We gotta give him a little lesson in obedience to a higher power—namely US! A few of those nuke busters might be enough to make him tremble in his pinto beans and show a little respect for the Chief—our Big George!

And why have we let stinking little Cuba off so easy? Isn't it about time we took care of that cigar totin' big shot? Struttin' around showin' the world that we can't tell him what to do—why do we stand for it? A coupla little ones on Havana and he'd sure see what "Super Power" is all about! And sick as he may be, he'd better mind his manners—and the U.S. of A!

Oh sure, I know a lotta softies will say that it's our tough shots that have been causin' the resentment and anger toward us, and causin' the terror stuff—hey, listen, I say look at Big George, Rummy, Wolfie, Chilly Dick and alla those guys—did we worry about what a bunch of little Muslims would think of us if we took over their land and happened to kill a few thousand of their people? And look how great that job is goin'!

Listen, we got a whole history of wars and takeovers and coups and bombing to defend—we can't suddenly care what the rest of the world thinks of us! Are we gonna let down our great patriotic Military Industrial Complex that's countin' on us for a few billion to cover their expenses?

Let's not forget that we're the Super Bully—I mean Super Power of the whole world! Bombs Away!

A HISTORY OF CREATIVE
WARMAKING NONE CAN EQUAL!

You have to give our presidents credit—eight wars—that's number 8—since WW II! What other country can make that claim? Number One in War! Doesn't that warm the cockles of your heart?

What other country can even come close? Not counting civil wars now, they're easy, angry factions with a history of friction, all right there in the same country, no long distances to travel and carry gigantic bombs and missiles and transport soldiers half way around the world in ships and planes, not to mention little things like carting food all over the world, trying to make sure it doesn't go bad—listen, that's how SPAM got started, good travel smarts!

And look at how thoughtful all of our warring presidents have been about making sure that our loyal soldiers get a real Christmas and Thanksgiving turkey dinner no matter how filthy and bloody and panicky they may be in some wild wooded land they never heard of whose strange looking citizens are always shooting at them or cutting their heads off. President Bush himself went all the way to Iraq to serve a real turkey dinner—well, he was actually holding a fake one himself for the photo op—for Christmas, or was it Thanksgiving? The point is—how many leaders in those pesky little civil wars actually go to serve a turkey dinner to their soldiers on Christmas—or maybe Thanksgiving? Not one I've ever seen pictured on CNN!

And let me say this—sure, there are lots of little wars between countries sharing a border, sharing water and all that ordinary stuff. But we don't have such easy ways to start a war—peaceable Canada above us and pretty little Mexico below, our only stormy borders being the oceans on both sides. Some might say that we were blest, living in peace with such nice neighbors.

But no! It would be too boring! And what of all of those weapons of mass destruction we've paid so much for and can boast of to the whole world? George

W is from Texas, a great big state, and his father had two fine wars, and he doesn't want to trail behind his Daddy! Only Jimmy Carter neglected all of that high-cost hardware, letting it get dusty. "Not one missile, not one bomb went out during my term of office to hurt anyone," he says. Is he boasting or apologizing?

He just wasn't creative enough! All of our presidents since WWII, except him and Eisenhower, have traveled far and wide to locate good spots for their military masterstrokes. Just five years after WWII, Truman began the saga by interfering in a civil war between North and South Korea . . . . I don't remember exactly, but I think one of them must have been involved in our Civil War, I don't know which side, I think the North, but Truman felt he had to pay back the debt, so he tried to stop the North part of Korea from planting communism onto the South, so he sent a few thousand of our young soldiers way over there to kill or be killed, and when some of them really did get killed, their parents were told "They died for their country."

This is what is always said to the parents or wives, and the government never says what would have happened to "their country" if they had NOT fought and died way around the world, but no doubt something terrible would have happened to "their country." Anyway, when General-President Eisenhower came into the Oval Office, he ended that war, and even though he was a fine general and could have waged a few dandy wars, he didn't have one, which plunged the Military Industrial Complex into a slough of despond—all that great battle know-how gone to waste!

This time was called "The Cold War," which sure is perplexing because all wars are pretty warm, even hot with powerful weapons. When President Kennedy came into the Oval Office, a lot of "advisors" were in Vietnam, like about anywhere in the world 'cause we're so smart other places want to share our wisdom. Some people said Kennedy was contemplating military action, but he actually said "Mankind must eliminate war, or war will eliminate mankind." But when Lyndon Johnson came into the White House following the shooting of President Kennedy, he saw that once more a North was trying to push communism onto a South, South Vietnam. Well, we had had eight years of peace—boring!—under President Eisenhower, and Kennedy hadn't lifted a shooting-finger for the Big Complex, so Johnson made the members of that war-eager group smile again as he rushed our young brave soldiers way over lands and seas to a brand new war. They say now that Lyndon was awfully upset when he heard, as he sat in his Oval Office, reports of thousands of our soldiers actually dying over there, and still the small Vietnamese fighters who lacked any of our wonderful bombs or even Agent Orange or Napalm were holding off our beautifully armed troops.

Well, Johnson was a Texas man, unafraid to show his operation scars, so he kept this battle going in spite of all the body bags and injured soldiers returning every day as he sat in his Oval Office. No sir, he kept sending our boys way over there to "fight for their country" in that lovely little land on the other side of the world that hardly anyone had ever heard of but now we had. But he finally gave up and went back to Texas and let Richard Nixon, who ran on a promise of ending the Vietnam War, take over. Lyndon's Defense Secretary, Robert McNamara, was glad to leave too.

By golly, there must be something about that Oval Office, because when he sat there Nixon tried to ignore the body bags and tons of angry war protesters. He turned patriotic and proud and sure he could end that distant scuffle with American victory, as always. Well, almost always, "Remember Korea?" some daring aide asked him. So, under a lot of pressure from irate citizens on different matters and the power of good liquor, Nixon finally threw in the towel, announced victory and brought the troops—those who were still alive—back home.

Nixon didn't talk much about figures in the war, but when former Secretary McNamara began to feel a little angst about the war, he announced that we lost more than 58,000 soldiers, and had killed 3,200,000 Vietnamese, innocents who had never done us any harm at all. Nixon had a few other matters, like being forced out of office, to worry about. But the Military officers sent patriotic letters to parents of those 58,000 plus dead soldiers saying that their sons had died "for their country." I don't know what the Vietnamese leaders said in letters to families of those 3,200,000 dead Vietnamese, but I guess they all knew that they died for their country all right. So Gerry Ford took over, no war on his agenda.

But for years we showed the Vietnamese our strength by leveling blockades against them to harm their chances for helpful trade because—put on your fantasy cap!—they weren't returning all of our MIA's! Who ever said we don't have chutzpah?

Democrat Jimmy Carter, another Southerner, was our next president, a man of peace who refused to start any war. So some of the patriotic men in the Military Industrial Complex that Ike warned us about were despondent again, but knew better times were coming when men more patriotic would take over that Oval Office. When Republican movie actor Reagan came swaggering in, the patriotic Complex held their breath—would he find a nice war for them? Well, he had one minor altercation with the little island of Grenada, but it was only a sample, nothing for the Big Complex to cheer about. Wasn't there something else somewhere in the world that needed the American touch—our great war machinery—to straighten out?

There sure was. Just a little south of Mexico was a stubborn country we had dominated for years and years—Nicaragua. Sure it had a nasty dictator, Somoza, but even Roosevelt had said with a smile over his cigarette holder, "He's an S.O.B.—but he's OUR S.O.B.!" Our companies pretty much ruled the land, but hey, we're all part of the same hemisphere, right?

But now a bunch of really determined citizens finally got together and, amazingly, ousted our political buddy, Somoza. They lost 40,000 of their revolutionary fighters, but what a triumph against a brutal dictator!

I mean, well, a triumph for Nicaraguans, sure, 'cause the new leaders, Daniel Ortega and other Sandinistas, eliminated polio within a year, opened clinics where residents had never seen a doctor, and were working hard to bring human rights and chances for work for their poorest. But wait—this wasn't beneficial for American companies who were depressed. So Reagan decided to take some action to stop those do-gooders he called "Commies," and their leader "That dirty little Commie in designer jeans!"

Well, Matinee Idol Ronnie felt that a lot of us might still remember the Vietnam War unhappily, so he and our fine Military Industrial Complex worked out a wily little scheme—hiring needy natives of a country nearby Nicaragua, like Honduras, pay and feed them, clothe and arm them with some of our finest weaponry. Have THEM, called Contra, instead of our own soldiers shoot and kill leaders of this new government, supervise them in destroying bridges, factories, and especially bombing buses and clinics, to undermine the new liberal government Reagan called "Commie."

Well, incredibly, very few Americans knew this clever, compassionate substitution for our troops was going on just south of the equator—how come? Because our media didn't care a fig about it! A little picture of a wounded child in a hospital in the New York Times, but why overdo it when our own soldiers were not involved? And that rascal Ronnie—didn't everybody just love him?—he thought that he would be appreciated for cutting back communism, whether it really WAS communism or not. At war's end, when he sent Americans to settle the peace and arrange the election, we actually paid the REAL Communist party to join the coalition of all 11 political parties to defeat the most popular party—the Sandinistas. Nicaraguans killed?—36,000. Not one American, except engineer, cyclist-clown Ben Linder, shot by a Contra while he was squatting at a possible site for drilling for water. Well, who knew much about that do-gooder anyway? Reagan never even mentioned him! What a brilliantly hidden war!

The first George Bush came into the White power House in a peaceful time, but soon found that his old buddy Noriega of Panama was not toadying up to him—so what could he do? Telling us that Noriega, was corrupting our youth by bombarding us with his drugs, Bush charged in there, destroyed six square blocks of homes and killed a few civilians along with a few U.S. soldiers—but hear this! Our fearless soldiers grabbed Noriega and swished him to Florida for trial and imprisonment! Against international law? A brazen show of our power? You bet! And George H. W. was cheered!

But that wasn't a big enough war for George One, and soon he was irked by another unsavory international big shot, Saddam Hussein of Iraq, who decided he wanted some of neighbor Kuwait's oil—hey, didn't I mention those cranky little border disputes? Not having any of our own, we want to share others', so Bush, with a few other countries, bravely led the soldiers into Kuwait and a little of Iraq to get old Saddam out of there stealing the oil that WE wanted to steal—er, own. No big deal! It was done in a few days, with some of Iraq's troops buried in the sand as they retreated. And if George the First had had a wimp factor, he got rid of it with two neat little wars! And he knew when to quit—so he didn't try to grab all of Iraq plus that testy leader Saddam, our former buddy.

Still, Bush One didn't want to appear to be an old softie, so to punish Saddam and make him look powerless, Bush saw that all of Iraq's water purification and sewage plants were knocked out, plants that keep water pure, especially crucial for elderly and children. So in the next ten years, about a half million elderly died, plus a million children, one of the reasons Osama has given for his attack on 9/11.

Another interesting surprise from that hasty little endeavor occurred when Sixty Minutes stunned its audience by presenting two soldiers plus a nurse from that war who were in mysterious weak conditions, many parts of their bodies not functioning—they believed it was caused by something they had not known was used in their artillery—depleted uranium, with a nuclear effect. When Iraqi women began having babies with three heads, tiny arms, all sorts of terrible defects, there seemed to be something serious here, but hey, maybe Bush didn't even know our military were using that stuff, and it can't be too serious 'cause we haven't seen much about it in our media, have we?

Well, next came Bill Clinton, who had a few non-military problems, made a few earnest trips to Israel to try to settle things down a little, and kept the sanctions against Iraq going so they never had a chance to clear up their water, as I mentioned above. Look, we didn't hear much about that in our newspapers, did we? Also, Clinton did a nice bit of bombing Iraq's no-fire zones when Saddam irritated him. He got involved in the plight of Kosovo, but didn't start a war of his own.

So, it was up to George Bush the Younger to get us into a dandy little war again—first going after the villain of 9/11, Osama bin Laden, hiding out in the tricky caves of Afghanistan. By gosh, young Bush did his best, bombing the colors out of those endless caves, killing a lot of horrified Afghans, women, children and men, about 1600 in all, but no luck in dropping in on Osama. So why waste our time and smart bombs on that barren land—forget about Osama and let Cheney, Wolfie and Rummy have their way—go after Saddam in Iraq! Yep George 2 did as they urged—actually, more or less commanded, especially Cheney who after all had had so much more international experience than young George. Well, after just a few months George said their Mission was Accomplished on that aircraft carrier, wearing that spiffy military uniform and looking chipper as a billy goat! Osama almost forgotten—but a lovely victory in Iraq!

Yes but, pretty soon things got out of hand, the darned Iraqis didn't seem to be welcoming us any more, a civil war breaking out to embarrass us, and in spite of Bush's saying over and over "I'm bringing peace to Iraq," and "democracy" and "I'm bringing freedom to the Middle East," it's pretty much a mess. He's still stuck there after four years, and deaths are adding up all over—more Americans killed over there than on 9/11—3,800 and still counting, and more than 750,000 Iraqis, none of whom had done us any harm. Not to mention the several million Iraqis scared to death to stay in their homes and fled to Syria or Jordan and are barely scraping by. Well, as Donald Rumsfeld succinctly noted, "Stuff Happens!"

Osama from 9/11? Bush says he isn't thinking much about him anymore—can you blame him, with the unsolvable quagmire in Iraq?

But anyway, still no sign of impeaching Bush II and his guiding hand—the icy hand of Dick Cheney; still not even Censure for them directed by Pelosi or Reid, only a weakened Republican party with a few more Republican senators being critical of the way the war's going without seeming to care if it hurts the president's feelings. And finally, some discontent and even anger on the part of our war-supporting public about how the numbers of our young American dead are growing, growing.

Now, this is quite a history of creative war making, equaled maybe only by the ancient Greeks or Romans. We have created a lovely empire through our wars and little coups, a history now being questioned by our own citizens and, it seems, by some of the people we thought we had under our ballistic thumbs. But not to worry—George W and Dick are still upbeat and determined to hang onto their "resolve," to "stay the course" till they kill all of the terrorists over there instead of "over here"—a never ending task since more are being provoked by our very presence on Muslim soil and our slaughtering of so many Muslims. Still, some say that Bush-Cheney will keep the war going nicely until the Democrats take over in 2009. Unless, of course, they happen to be impeached.

Yes, there is quite a little build-up of fault-finding now, but not a word of complaint from even one member of the warm-hearted Military-Industrial-Complex! Way to go!

THE GREAT DREAMERS

Once upon a time, dear children, there was a gathering of dreamers, men of great and grandiose dreams who lived in a country of majestic mountains, green valleys and cities of beauty and bad air. And lo, these men, who had already achieved much in the way of wealth and privilege for their families, dreamed dreams of great imagination and glory in lands far far across the oceans, dreams for the benefit of a Higher Power and their beloved homeland of spacious farms, lakes, and tax breaks for the richest among them.

And so, my dear children, they formed a bond, a sort of club like one you may belong to for playing games or baking cookies. Dick and Donald and William and Paul and Douglas met to assure each other that yes, if there is a God in Heaven, their dreams would come true! But, my dear children, the greatest plans of mice and men can often go to pot, and so now their hopes and dreams were detoured by a president not of their philosophy, and lo, they were much aggrieved. So aggrieved were they when this president was elected a second time, they shot off furious golf balls and spewed language that would shock your mommies! Still, devoted to their Higher Power and each other, some of these dreamers went fearlessly to the House of White to visit this president, whose name was Bill, and entreated him to achieve their finest dreams.

But this president said with a chuckle and snort, "Are you guys outta your gourd? No, I will not invade Iraq and take out Saddam! Look, I am hanging onto those sanctions that prohibit them from importing chlorine to make their water nice and clean, water your pals destroyed, remember? And I am doing a little patriotic bombing now and then, but that's it! So toodloo!" Lo, the men left with hearts deep in a blue funk, bad name-calling on their lips. Somehow, kiddies, they were not satisfied that a million little kids like you and their grandmothers would die in ten years from that nasty dirty water that President Bill never worried about, though he had a sweet little girl of his own who had nice water and milk and ginger ale whenever she was thirsty—I bet you do too!

But so discouraged were Don and Dick and Paul and Scooter and William and Richard and Jeb that they broke down and wept copiously. Then they met often to scrupulously plot to bring in one of their own to the head of their country of great scientific triumphs and no national healthcare. And so, kiddies, their plotting and planning, stacks of lovely green stuff and an affectionate Supreme Court did indeed achieve a grand goal—one of their own philosophy, little experience and open to nutty ideas was elected president of their land of beauty, power and great halls of learning for the lucky few who could afford them.

And, oh, my children, how these dreamers of great dreams rejoiced! Now, they declared loudly to each other, they could plan their great actions for the Higher Power! The new president's brother Jeb, loyal to their dreams, had already accomplished a great feat—one of his fellow dreamers, Dick was now vice-president. The new president, a stranger to his new big city, said "Sure, Dick, bring in a bevy of your buddies—Donald, Scooter, Paul, Douglas, John, Zalmay and Richard for starters. Is it okay if I bring in Karl?" All they coveted now, little children, was an excuse to begin their grand adventure far across the seas of reshaping what is called the Middle East. Their new president listened to them with friendly mien, lousy judgment, and a small breathy chuckle.

One day, my little cherubs, children like you were listening to this new president read a nice little story about a goat. Suddenly, a man came into the schoolroom and whispered into the president's ear. He sat in the small chair looking confused, perhaps because he saw a big word on the page he could not read. But later that day the people of his land learned that a very bad thing had happened—some planes flew into two tall towers and they fell very fast to the ground, with many people dying therein, and a third tower nearby also collapsed that evening even though no plane flew into that one, which is a very interesting mystery, isn't it?

So now, my dear little listeners, Paul and Dick and Donald and William and Scooter hugged each other in joy and told the president of little experience and less compassion that now they just had to invade Iraq and take out Saddam, because of "9/11." The new president of very little experience or deep thoughts chatted with his pal Karl, and then went to bed chanting over and over, "Since 9/11, since 9/11," and yea, boy! He did say it very well, adding, when on TV of many watchers, a frown of profound and Karl-positioned resentment. And so, although both the President and the man who talked to soldiers, Donald, said there was no connection between Saddam of Iraq and 9/11, they asked the House of Government Helpers if they could start the war. Wow, kids, hold onto your seat belts—even the Clinton side of Helpers said "Sure, why not? We haven't had a war in almost ten years!" And lo, babies, three other senators who wanted to be president also voted FOR this sill-tilly war! Listen, kids, who wants to sound unpatriotic, huh? Not these bas—uh, not these ambitious smarties!

And thus began the cruel and embarrassing war against that little country of innocent people who had never harmed us at all! Our brave pilots flew over many homes like yours where little children, like you, were sleeping, and dropped humongous bombs, crushing the children and their mommies and daddies to death! LOUSY DAMNED SOBS WHO DON'T CARE A FIG ABOUT HUMAN LIVES! Uh, excuse me, kiddies, uh, sorry!

Now, children, although a famous beloved general and president said often how he hated war, calling it "brutal, futile and stupid!" many fine people of your lovely land of gardens and lakes and factories making more killing machines than ever in history, accepted the war and deaths of our smiling young soldiers and of the unseen Iraqi people never shown by Jim Lehrer—but hang on a minute—IT'S ALL CHANGING NOW1 A few years TOO LATE, people are mad at that head-shaking president and that club of dreamers called the Project for a New American Century surrounding him in the big House of White, even the same Government Helpers who at first had said, "Another war? Sure, why not?"

So now, kiddies, where the hell are we, huh? The Great Dreamers got their dream all right—a nightmare now—for the Higher Power of Oil! That's exactly what a brilliant man of great Greenspan said. Only a few today, like William of a Standard of Weekly News and Deceits, still think the nightmare, quagmire, hell in Iraq can be solved neatly. Don, Paul and Scooter are gone now, and a bit shy in defending their dream of destruction and death. Even Dick the Unseen is more and more invisible, though when abruptly caught on camera still defends the "quagmire" with admirable duplicity.

Okay then, Kids, what's the lesson here? Anyone? The little girl with the pink ribbon in her hair? Huh? . . . "War is bad, and we shouldn't ever have another one" Very good. Go tell it to the men in the big House of White, and to the lazy, weak-livered and corruptible Government Helpers who said, "A new war? Sure, why not?"

That's the end of the story, till the next war, kiddies.

A NICE SURPRISE FOR MALIKI

I know just how Nuri al-Maliki must have felt when he was told that George Bush was arriving in five minutes—just as I would if I learned that my mother-in-law was coming in five minutes—oh my God! Can I do the vacuuming—No! Wash the dishes in the sink—No! Tell my husband to take the load of clean laundry off her bed in the guest room—and put clean towels in the bathroom! Yikes! Check the litter box—My God! I hear her taxi! You go to the door—I'll put on a nice dress!

What a horrible surprise! For both of us! I bet Maliki did a little Middle Eastern cursing, and muttered "Allah be praised, these Americans think they can come and go whenever they please, so here comes one more takeover. I suppose he wants to see just how their big embassy, biggest in the world, is going—is it big enough?"

I wonder what Maliki did first—put on a clean sheet? Comb his hair? Reach for a clean turban or put on a red, white and blue tie? Rush into a prayer session? I bet he prayed "Allah be praised, and help me hold back my Muslim fury that the big Bush was not courteous enough to let me know sooner—just look at my desk—what a mess! Okay, I'll stuff these folders and papers into this drawer. Ibrahim, put a clean towel in the men's bathroom! And a new tape in the crazy little machine—we can't be too careful with these pushy Americans who cannot tell truth from falsehood!

Allah be praised! I hear his little chuckle right now—Ah, Mr. President! What a lovely surprise! If I knew you were coming I'd have baked a rice cake! Ha ha! You are looking well in spite of your sinking polls, and is Laura with you? Oh, too bad, such a lovely lady. And how about Rummy, such a uh, calm and confident man . . . no? Send my regards. And how was your ride from the airport? It can be quite . . . exciting—oh, you chose to take a helicopter right here to the super-power-safe Green zone, how clever of you!

However, you missed a fine stretch of our fine city, and I would have commanded our soldiers to guide you through Baghdad, and have seen that the dead bodies and rubble from your fine bombing of our buildings were cleared away.

I am sure you will want to meet our ministers, all in position now—how about tomorrow morning, after prayers, say 10 o'clock? . . . oh, you are leaving tonight? Only four hours? Ah well, I shall have to hurry—luckily I have a meeting shortly with Sunni clerics, you will find this very interesting . . . You don't think so? Yes, of course, I will set up a meeting instead with our ministers after prayers.

Then perhaps, so you can gain, as you say you are seeking, a comprehensive view of the land you have paid so much to occupy, a little stroll down the streets of our great city where you will surely meet some of your fine soldiers, those who have not been killed yet, and also some of our own citizens who would be most . . . uh, eager to meet you—only the men, of course, women and children prefer to stay inside to avoid being raped, robbed, killed or kidnapped.

No? A little too warm for a walk? Perhaps, though it is only 121 degrees today. But you do look a little warm—the Quixotic electricity is not working today, so neither is our fine U.S. air conditioning. How about a coke?

THIS PRESIDENT'S GOT GUTS!

He's come under a lot of fierce criticism lately, but you've really got to hand it to George Bush for guts—what other president, while he's sending young Americans to get killed or have their arms and legs torn off, would have the guts to put a whoopee cushion on Karl Rove's chair so when Karl sat down the whole Cabinet could have a good laugh? We're talking about FUN here! So much less FUN with Karl gone now!

How about the guts the guy has to keep saying—through four years of a ghastly war with at least 750,000 Iraqis dead, whole families crushed to death under our bombs—over and over, "I'm bringing peace to Iraq!" You think that's EASY?

And what about the press conference when asked about his shameful war, saying solemnly, soulfully, "The Iraqi people want peace, they want to live in a peaceful environment!" Now, that takes unbelievable GUTS!

Speaking of guts, how about the reporters who heard those words and didn't laugh or scream—"Peace? No! You've given them a long criminal WAR, you ***!" And how about reporters there who have been to Iraq and seen the unbearable horror for soldiers and Iraqis, but when Bush made a sour little joke they actually LAUGHED at it! Hearty laughter that prevented another sharp question! Is that patient, forgiving GUTS or what?

The cocky president smiled appreciatively while he was killing a few hundred more in Iraq at that very moment. He's got GUTS to spare!

A reporter asked about the way Bush's been referring to Iran, similar to the build-up for war with Iraq—planning war with Iran now? The Pres answer: he knew "some weapons in Iraq that are killing our fine soldiers come from Iran," and he (jaw-tight determination) was going to protect his fine soldiers—avoiding the question ALTOGETHER! The next person called on and the nexts had the guts to FORGET the non-answer to the question du jour! That took journalistic GUTS!

And speaking of guts, what about the Senatorial presidential candidates—John Edwards, Joe Biden and Chris Dodd—all having the GUTS to say their votes FOR the Iraq War were a MISTAKE, gee, they're real sorry. That takes Campaign-Smart GUTS!

They ask why that darned Hillary won't say that SHE made a little mistake and SHE'S sorry too! She just says in her high-volume, don't-miss-a-word-I-say-voice that the "president LIED to me!" and if she had been president then—"We would not have GONE TO WAR!" Actually, Bill must have told her when Cheney and the Project for a New American Century asked him to invade Iraq and take out Saddam in 1998—but still she voted FOR the war—and has the guts to NOT say she's sorry!

A lot of guts highlighted the Scooter Libby trial—even the guts to still call himself by the kiddies' name "Scooter"! Again, our warm-hearted president, dismissing the problems that leaking the position of Joe Wilson's wife, Valerie Plame, caused her, thoughtfully spoke of "how hard this verdict is for Scooter's wife." Not a word about how hard it is for thousands of military wives now facing their young husbands' deaths, or adjusting to their husbands' mutilation and physical or mental changes—I tell you, this president, whether he actually won the last two elections or not, the guy has GUTS you can't overlook, even if you wish you could!

Anyway, Scooter's wife didn't have to worry—she just knew that George W would pardon loyal old Scooter!

And how about the GUTS to keep complaining about the danger of Iran's Ahmadinejad's sure power for terrorism, a country we helped old Saddam attack when he was our buddy during Reagan years, and now we have ourselves TERRORIZED two MILLION Iraqis to leave their homeland—how's this for GUTS?

And when he's not too busy excusing lack of armor in Iraq or scandals in vets hospitals, Bush Two, while the world gasps at unverified charges of torture and suicides in Guantanimo, has the guts to charge other countries, such as Egypt, with "They lack good human rights!' This guy's got a record of all time—you can't deny it—for great PRESIDENTIAL GUTS! And, God help us—his GUTS aren't ended YET!

CONDOLEEZZA RICE'S PRESS CONFERENCE

GOOD AFTERNOON, PRESS. I AM DELIGHTED TO BE HERE TO BRING YOU ALL OF THE INVALUABLE, DIAMETRICALLY OPPOSITIONED EVALUATIONS OF OUR AESTHETICALLY VICIITUDINOUS AND ALLEGRO NON TROPPO INTERVENTIONS OF OUR PRESIDENT AROUND THE WORLD TO HEROICALLY AND NONHEROICALLY PUSH DEMOCRACY DOWN THEIR THROATS. I SHALL BE ALMOST VICARIOUSLY DELIGHTED TO ATTACK YOUR QUESTIONS, QUESTIONS OF MULTITUDINOUS AND PUSILANEOUS INTENTABILITYOUSNESS ABOUT THE COURAGEOUS MAN IN THE WHITE PAVILION. I AM DISTASTEFULLY HERE TO BRING YOU ALL OF THE INVALUABLE, DIAMETRICALLY OPPOSED AND FRUCTUOUSLY, POSITIVELY AND AESTHETICALLY VICIITUDINOUS AS WELL AS NONCALAMATIOUS INTERVENTIONS AROUND THIS PALTRY AND PRETENTIOUSLY PREVALENT WORLD TO COHERENTLY AND BENEVOLENTLY PUSH DEMOCRACY DOWN THE THROATS OF THE MIDDLE EAST.

I AM RESIGNED TO RESPOND TO YOUR MULTITUDINOUSLY INANE QUESTIONS ABOUT THE STUPENDITIOUS ACTIONS OF YOUR PRESIDENT, MY PRESIDENT, THE WORLD'S PRESIDENT, RESPECTED GLORIOUSLY AND SURREPTITIOUSLY BY THE WORLD NO MATTER HOW MANY PEOPLE HE HAS TO CAPTURE, HUMILIATE, AND TORTURE WATERBOARDICIOUSLY.

SO, GOOD AFTERNOON, MEDIA, I AM DELIGHTED TO BE HERE TO BRING YOU ALMOST ALL OF THE INFORMATION YOU SO CRUDELY DEMAND IN UTTER DENIAL OF MY BRILLIANCE

AND DEDICATION TO THE MAN WE ALL RESPECT FOR HIS INTELLIGENCE AND DEPTHS OF WISDOM, YOUR PRESIDENT AND . . . MY PRESIDENT. FOR HE IS A MAN OF DEEP AND INVISIBLE WISDOM, INTEGRITY, COURAGE, STICKTUOSITY AND BRAINDATIONESS NO MATTER HOW COLD-HEARTED, DUMB AND IGNORANT HE MAY APPEAR ON TV.

HE IS ALSO A MAN OF EXTREMIST COMPASSIONOSITY . . . DO NOT THINK THAT HE HAS NO COMPASSIONOSITY ABOUT THE CASUALTIES IN IRAQ, OF OUR DISASTROUSLY INNOCENT AND NOT SO INNOCENT YOUNG MEN, WHO RECKLESSLY SIGNED UP FOR THIS MARVELOUSLY EXTRANEOUIS WAR THAT THE GREASTEST MINDS IN THE WORLD CALL, MOST PHILOSOPHICALLY, ONE HELL OF A MESS! BUT OUR PRESIDENT, YOUR PRESIDENT, YOURS, YOURS TOO . . . AND MINE . . . IS EVEN MORE UPSET SINCE KARL HAS LEFT US AND THERE'S NO ONE, I REPEAT, NO ONE FOR GEORGE TO PLAY HIS DEAR WHOOPEE CUSHION GAME WITH! THANK YOU ALL FOR BEING SO AGITATO, ALLEGRO AND OCCASIONALLY MOLTO FORTISSIMO WITH ME THIS AFTERNOON. I BELIEVE I HAVE ANSWERED ALL OF YOUR INSIGNIFICANTLY VACUOUS QUESTIONS WITH MY TRADITIONAL VIRTUOUSITY AND DEVIOUSLY DEVILISH DIVERSIONS. ADDIOS, ADIEU AND GUTEN RIDDENCE!

BUSH ONE-LINERS BETTER THAN LENO OR LETTERMAN!

And How Well he Gets Away with them!

As a long-time Democrat—for 55 years—and a freelance writer and writing teacher, I just have to admire the language skills of my president, George W. Bush.

Because I have never known any president so clever with words! He uses words, phrases, nouns and adjectives more brilliantly than any politician in my historic time.

Note a sentence he has been repeating since the day the Iraq War began: "I'm bringing PEACE to Iraq!" and in time generously switching to first person plural, perhaps including the soldiers he sent way over there: "We're bringing peace to Iraq!" Now, really, how many other presidents who were sending our innocent young soldiers to a distant land to bomb, shoot and kill innocent civilians and get horribly wounded themselves or maybe even killed, how many of them would have thought of saying such a sentence with a straight face—AND getting away with it!

Who objected? Nobody! Not one Democrat—not Ted Kennedy, not Robert Byrd! Not Nancy Pelosi! Not one TV anchor or talk show guy—not Chris Matthews! Not columnist Maureen Dowd! Y'see (a little intro I borrowed from Bush), bombs were falling on private homes, a man stood on CNN and said that when he returned after a trip he found his home totally destroyed, his wife and five little children crushed to death under the bombardment of bricks and cement! What horror! What terrorism—for them, not for us sitting safely at home and watching our president on TV saying with a gentle smile—"We're bringing peace to Iraq!"

Now, true, some of those Iraqi Muslims may not have seen this gift of peace coming from the world's super-armed power, obscured as it may have been by the smoke and flames of our smart bombs. Even a few unobservant Americans may have missed the arrival of peace to Iraq, their view blunted by words and faces on TV of Kofi Anan, the Pope, the Methodist bishop and those dang peace activists who keep offering the words of Republican general and President Dwight Eisenhower, saying how he "hates war, its brutality, futility, stupidity!" So our Pres kept reiterating that happy sentence every day, every evening when he appeared anywhere—"We're bringing peace to Iraq!" Amazing.

Then suddenly bringing peace just to Iraq wasn't enough—Bush made a smooth variation—"Y'see, I'm bringing peace to the Middle East!" Good news for the whole Middle East! Well, there may have been a little skepticism here and there . . . Iran was rumored to be sending a few fighters to help the beleaguered Iraqis, and it was hard to hear even a few words of encouragement to us from any country in the world except England—well, even the British citizens weren't cheering Tony Blair in the streets while calling him "Bush's poodle!"

But ever resourceful, Bush pulled another winner out of his baseball cap—"I'm bringing FREEDOM to Iraq! Y'see, they've never had our freedom, so now I'm bringing them freedom, yep, FREEDOM! Y'see, God wants everybody in the whole world to have freedom!" Sure, 20 or 30 thousand Iraqis who were killed that week in our bombs and missiles missed this great chance for freedom, but those who survived must be happy as clams! . . . well, maybe not all of them, since so many are fighting against us, true, but aren't there always a few soreheads?

I'm just as impressed with "I'm bringing freedom to the Middle East!" OUR freedom, freedom through war! Talk about originality! I bet the whole Middle East was just waiting for this joyfil warning—I mean message!

Some will say that it isn't George who is creating this great wordcraft, it's Karl Rove. Maybe so, and he deserves credit—but who is pulling off these terrific daily one-liners with Jay Leno confidence and bravura, not a glance of guilt? George W. himself! How can any writer not be impressed?

Peace through war! Freedom through occupation!

Brilliant! Unbelievable! Only in the good old US of A!

PART 3
DRAMA

JIM LEHRER ON NEWS HOUR READS NAMES OF IRAQI DEAD

Girl of about 19 is watching TV set, of which audience sees only its side; the voice of newsman Jim Lehrer speaks.

Lehrer: This is Jim Lehrer. Now, as the names and information about the latest Iraqi deaths are received, we present their faces, ages, and where they were from: First, the women: Rana Halid, 17, of Baghdad;

Girl: (She calls to her mother): Gee, Mom, she's even younger than I am—she's so pretty—was so pretty.

Lehrer: Sajida Yaseen, 76, of Tikrit; Suha Ahlam; 36, also of Tikrit.

Girl's mother comes, stands by her daughter's chair, then sits nearby.

Lehrer: Amal Nassen, 4 hears old, of Baghdad.

Girl and mother: Oh, my God!

Girl: A tiny little kid, Mom, so cute—we killed her, Mom! One of our soldiers killed her!

Mother: Yeah, yeah, that's what war is for, killing . . .

Lehrer: Siham Alatar, 5, and Janay Alatar, 7, and their mother, Ruma Alatar, 35. of Diyala.

Mother and girl exclaim ad lib: Isn't that awful! Oh my God!

Girl: I wonder if there's any family left—

Mother: Probably the father, poor guy . . .

Lehrer: Now the men who have died recently, as we have received their pictures: Abbas Nouri, 51, and Mostafa Sabri, 48, both of Karbala.

Mother: Just your father's age, 48.

Girl: Yeah . . .

Lehrer: Muhammed Obu Omen, 22, and Karim Aziz, 19, both of Samarra.

Girl: My age, Mom, I could've gone out with them, nice looking guys . . . gee . . .

Mother: There seem to be a lot of them tonight, more than usual.

Lehrer: And Kahlid Mussahn, 13, Jakir Mussahn, 11, and Hussan Mussahn, 7, and their mother, Sura Mussahn, 41, all of Mosul.

Girl: My God, Mom—that's like the father we saw on CNN last week, who lost his whole family, remember? He stood there telling us how he came home from a trip and when he got to his house . . . .

As she recalls the incident of the man who lost his family, the man appears and begins speaking to the audience as the Girl's voice diminishes on the man's words; she and the mother sit quiet as the man speaks emotionally.

Man: I came home from a little trip, but when I got to my house—it was gone! A pile of rubble! And my five children, my wife—all killed by your bomb! All crushed to death when my house was blown up and smashed down on them—why? Why did you do this to me? And to the others on my street, their homes, their families all destroyed by your horrible bombs—why? What did we ever do to you that you come here and kill our children, our mothers and fathers? How would you feel if this happened to you? How can I go on living!

His voice softens as he exits slowly, and girl resumes speaking.

Girl:—and he said his life was over, over, his whole family gone, all those little kids . . . (she is teary)

Mother: (rising, touches her daughter briefly before she exits) I know, I know, Honey, we have to stop all these wars, even Eisenhower said so, the general president. Listen, let's turn off the TV, you come and help me with dinner, okay?

Girl: (turns off TV) Okay, before he reads the names of American soldiers killed next . . .

She rises and exits, wiping her eyes.

End of scene

The man who describes his losses appeared on CNN shortly after the Iraq war began, describing this incident.

SAM AND BUSH HAVE A CHAT— A DREAM ?

Bush is seated at his desk, writing. He looks up as he hears someone entering. Sam enters wearing his red, white and blue high hat; Bush stands briefly to shake his hand.

Bush: Come right in, Sam, how've you been?

Sam: Could be better. How about you?

Bush: Could be better—Iraq still a mess, New Orleans still a mess, terrible fires in California, more hurricanes . . .

Sam: No health care for a few million people, winter's coming, and some people won't be able to heat their homes—

Bush: Scandals erupting, commission hearings, all kinds of inquiries . . .

Sam: Halliburton getting more no-bid contracts—

Bush: I didn't hear about that—

Sam: It was in all of the papers, George.

Bush: That's why I didn't hear about it. I'll have to ask Cheney.

Sam: He's the one who sets it up!

Bush: Sam, I've met with my Cabinet, told them we're headin' in a new direction.

Sam: Good luck. But hey, George, about big Katrina and the fires and all—our smartest scientists say that it's due to global warming—Katrina was a real warning, George.

Bush: Really? Dick says that global warming had nothing to do with it, and making companies change their habits would be bad for our economy, see?

Sam: He would say that. See, George, when the oceans get too warm, breezes grow stronger, pick up speed and lambaste the shores. Oceans are rising because of the glaciers melting.

George: I respect what you're sayin' cause you've been around a long time. And uh, if you don't mind me asking, how are you comin' with your—uh, bad habit?

Sam: (joyfully) My bombing? A lot better! Thanks to you—stlowin' the war in Iraq and bringing in those Middle East leaders and old Desmond Tutu and Mandela, Jimmy too. But I still worry—only two presidents since WWII, Carter and Eisenhower, had no wars.

George:(looks worried) I wish I'd been one of them . . .

Sam: I'm so worn out from all those years of bombing, I'd like to make a law to ban it.

Bush: That's it, Sam—a law against war, like Japan's—unless we get invaded!

Sam: Great idea!

George: I'll have to talk to—

Sam: Not Cheney! And don't call Wolfie or Rummy! A law to end war . . . like witch burning and duels! Ancient habits are sure hard to kick! (He stands to lave)

Bush: Thanks, Sam. *D*rop in any time.

Sam: Sure will, George, and give my regards to God! (Goes off)

Bush: (Begins to write) Call Condi . . . call uh . . . Ted Kennedy, Bob Byrd . . . Ron Paul, (chuckle) old peace guy from Texas, Dennis Kucinich . . . (chuckles) he'll sure be surprised to hear from me . . . how about Chuck Hagel? . . . and . . . Cindy Sheehan!

End of scene

WORKING ON THE BIG BOMBS AND DOWN FROM THE SKY

Two almost works of fiction

I'm a hard working woman, just 41 years old, and a single mom. Right now, I don't even know where my husband and father of my three children is. No payment from him in 10, almost 11 months. I hafta work to support them, no question about it.

At first I tried being a waitress, I'd done that before I was married. But the hours are too long, the pay too little, I couldn't support my kids on that. So, what to do . . . well, I knew about this war plant not very far from my house . . . my priest didn't like it so close, but he finally gave up protesting. I met a woman at church one Sunday, a new woman, a little older than me, and we got to talking after church, she didn't know any people around here, but she came here to get a good job—at the war plant, and she makes $16 an hour!

She said they were looking for more help, so I decided to go there and apply for a job—$16 an hour would be lots better than the $6.50 plus tips I was getting at the little restaurant around the corner. And I had a car, old and ugly, but it goes. So I went over to the place as soon as I could, and I got a job—15.50 an hour! Well, I'm a big woman, five feet eight, 175 pounds. They asked me if I have any health problems, and if I have plenty of energy. I said sure, so now I'm helping to make bombs, BIG bombs. The B21 ones right now, but they're planning on a new bigger one in a few months.

Sure it was sort of funny at first . . . just to see the size of these big jobs—I have to swing one on a heavy wire, it takes three of us to pull it along, then my job is to coat it with some stuff, like a glue, so I have to wear gloves and a mask 'cause of the fumes. And they always have air conditioning blowin' so I guess it's pretty safe, and you get to take breaks four times a day, better than at the old lunch place all right. You oughta see the size of these big rooms where they make these things—the whole plant covers three blocks, with separate buildings for the stuff they make. At first, my very first day, I was kinda scared just to see the size of those babies . . . I mean, the ones I work on are at least seven feet long, and fat too . . . the guy I work for, he says one a these if they drop it on some street can destroy eight or nine homes or four or five big buildings like churches.

Well, I have to be on my feet all day, but I was used to that, you don't get much chance to sit down workin' tables, so I think I can take it, though pushing those big ones around to where I can do the coating isn't easy, and he says after a while I'll have to do more of the pushin' myself. So far, the other workers there, most of them are women, too, in my division, but they say in some of the divisions they're all men, and it's real secret stuff.

So far I haven't told my priest, and not my children, no sirree, they might ask too many questions, especially Eddie, my oldest, almost 15, and such a nice gentle little guy, always askin' questions about the war over there in Iraq, see, 'cause he hears about it on TV and his history teacher has them write about it and all hat. No, he wouldn't be so glad to have me workin' on those bombs . . . I can't say I'm real happy makin' those big ones, seems the company always has business ready, I mean the government, and the best part of it is that I get good health insurance now, for me and the kids, that's the best thing so far, and the pay. God, I can actually take us all out for a nice Chinese dinner once in a while, they love Chinese food. Some day I'll hafta tell Father Tom about it, but not yet, I know he won't like the idea of me helpin' to make big bombs to kill innocent people, like he talks about sometimes in his homily. Well, so be it, I hafta support my kids. That's all.

High in the Sky

I've been an Air Force pilot for a lotta years now, good pay, good digs and all that, especially since I became a bomber. But somethin' happened on my last coupla missions over there . . . . usually they came at night, all I could see was the gigantic explosion, dark as the night, and some red fire, that's all I could see, actually so far below I couldn't see what the hell I was hitting, I just took the orders when to drop the stuff, that's all. But for some reason this one time, we were ordered to take a day-time hit . . . and this time right after the big one dropped, before I dropped the next one, I got a view of what we had hit—a long row of houses, hardly anything left standing but piles of smoking rubble, these great piles of burning hills that had been houses—how about the people inside? Jesus, I felt sick to my stomach—I threw up, which held back the next one, and they were yelling, "Go ON, drop the next one! What the hell's the matter? Christ, you're sick?" Yeah, I was sick, so they told my trainee, a kid only 19, to do the next one. Well, he was slow, not quite sure what he was doing, and I was too busy throwing up my guts to help him, so we missed that chance.

The pilot circled around and ordered the same hit again maybe a little farther south, I think, but I was too sick to respond so the kid came through this time and I just sat there throwing up and feeling pains in my chest and my stomach, I thought maybe I was dying, I had these awful pains and I couldn't even see straight . . . I passed out, that was my good luck . . . I didn't wake up till we landed and they had to carry me out and a medic hurried up to me . . . they were yellin' "Take him to the hospital! Get him on the next flight!" I should have stayed asleep, gone to Germany to our doctors there, they might have been easier on me . . . but I woke up, stopped throwing up, and slept all day, then told my captain I couldn't do it anymore.

Well, he's a stubborn little guy, told me we were snort of bombers, I could take the next day off, sleep, eat carefully, and be on duty the next night. I said softly that "I can't do it anymore," and he said, "Sure you can, just get a good night's sleep," and he walked off. I went to sleep, ate a good breakfast the next morning and packed up my clothes, went to his office with my bag, and told the lieutenant on duty that I wanted to make the next shift home, I was through. He laughed a little, then said, "What the hell are you saying? You can't just—go home! We're at war here!"

When I got to the captain again, he was really pissed. "Who the hell do you think you are? You think we all like being here? I got a new baby at home, I haven't even seen it—three months old—what the hell do you think you're asking for? You want a few days in Kuwait? I'll give you that, but you gotta come back and get up there, we got our orders, see?"

I sat down on the one little chair in his neat little office. "Uh uh, I'm quitting, right now, sorry, Dick. I want out. We're makin' a mess of this war, you know it, I know it, we all know it, and whatever it means for me, I can't take it any more—maybe hafta go to prison, that's okay. I'm not flyin' any more." I started walking out, and he went bananas. I went back to my mess, had some coffee and that morning they had nice fresh donuts . . . I couldn't believe how happy I feltI, I should have been scared shitless, but I felt cheerful, even began laughing. One of the guys asked me what the hell I was laughing about.

I said, "I've just stopped killing babies. Probably going to prison instead."

So I'm back in the States, waiting for my hearing, I'm at a stinky little army camp in Florida, waiting for someone to take my case. They won't let me go home to see my mom, she's got some new health problems, but they don't care . . . well, whatever, I'm not in the air . . . got some pretty tough nightmares, like a lot of us will have for years, I guess, years and years . . . .

SCENE FROM "GOD TALKS TO GEORGE BUSH"

God leans down toward the world, looks upset.

God: George! George . . . can you hear me? (He listens to hear George's voice) Oh, my own heavens—you're in an airplane, the one place you cannot hear me . . .

Oh, my dear son, how eager some of my humans are to plunge into the evil of war! Not a sigh of concern for the human beings barely grown commanded to destroy and kill, and have their lovely arms and legs torn off their bodies as they scream . . . or lose the very breath of life I have given them . . . and then their loved ones scream!

I must not turn aside from these unfeeling humans, for the fault must be partly mine . . . Ah, yes, there they are . . . what are they saying . . . could I have been mistaken in my perceptions and fears . . .

As God speaks to the men addressed, he pauses for their responses between his phrases.

Richard, Donald, Paul, Lewis, William, I beseech you to listen to my plea, as your leader so has . . . . do you hear me, there in my good earth . . . . must I beg you to open your ears and hearts to me now, your God and creator, maker of heaven and earth . . . . oh, my good son, if you were only here again to preach the gospel of love to these ice-laden men! I cannot reach them because their minds are shuttered to all but their own avidity and ambition . . . . once more, you men inflamed with power; hear my entreaty for peaceable efficacy!

They cannot, will not hear, mendacious men clothed in fascination of acquisition and death; the sweet air of orchids and moonlight they breathe greedily, but stifle in their young and all ages far away—distance diminishes scruple and unravels the warp of humanity . . .

(Despairing now) O my saints, you innocents whispering in the cacophony of this world, centuries of time have ripened talents and spoiled the souls of men . . . progress only in deceit, devastation . . . and man's inhumanity to man! (almost sobbing now) How could this happen . . . my ideals, my dreams . . . how I have failed, and now all is hopeless and all I can do . . . is weep! (He breaks down and sobs)

End of scene, end of the play

BOMBAHOLICS ANONYMOUS, ADDICTION SCENE

Scene is a reception room for welcoming persons with addictions. A receptionist sits at a desk. Sign on the wall: ADDICTION CENTER—ALL ADDICTIONS WELCOME

Receptionist is writing at her desk. In comes a man smoking furiously, gasping for air.

Receptionist: Good morning. (brushes away the smoke from her face, coughs)

Smoker: Is it? It's just my usual morning—cough, light up, gasp—shout "You're killin' yourself! Stop smoking!" (big spasm of coughing.) But I can't! I'm hopeless!

Receptionist: There's always hope, that's why we're here. Just sign your name here, and go right into our emergency room! (she points)

Smoker signs name quickly, walks while puffing off stage.

The Drinker staggers in, looking around as if he can't see where he is. Receptionist rises.

Receptionist: Try to make it over here and sit down, okay? And, what is your problem?

Drinker lurches and looks around, sees the chair and lunges perilously toward it.

Drinker: Huh? (tries to think) My problem? (shakes his head quickly) My problem? (veers left and right, forward; receptionist pushes him upright.)

Receptionist: Do you have a little problem with alcohol perhaps?

Drinker: No, a HUGE problem—my wife has left me, I lost my job! I'm hopeless! (cries)

Receptionist: There's always hope, that's why we're here. So why don't you try to write your name here. (Drinker struggles to write his name. Receptionist helps him up and guides him into next room) Fine. We're going to our Emergency Room right now! (off)

A man with white beard enters, wearing a red, white and blue suit, holding his star-bright tall hat. He looks around, wonders if he is in the right place, sees the big sign, nods.

New man: Oh yeah. this is the place. (sits)

Receptionist returns, sits at her desk, smiles at him,

Receptionist: Hi there, how are you today?

New man: I'm never sure. I have a bad habit, can't seem to lick it, year after year, century after century! (He slumps into the chair, groans)

Receptionist: Well, are you a workaholic, an alcoholic, a chocoholic—

New man: None of those little things! (stands) I'm a bombaholic!

Receptionist: (a bit flustered) A . . . bombaholic?

New man: Right! I just can't stop bombing! All over the world, anywhere, any time! (desperately, grabbing onto her) I need help!!

Receptionist: I can see that. Sit down, please, try to calm down. (She pats his shoulder)

New man: "Calm down"? That's my problem—I get annoyed, stirred up, mad, and I start bombing! (sits) It's hopeless!

Receptionist: It's never hopeless, that's why we're here. What is your name, please?

New man: Sam. My name's Sam.

Receptionist: And your last name, please?

New man: Sam is my last name, my first name is Uncle.

Receptionist: (politely, as she writes) Uncle . . . Sam.

Sam: That's right, but everybody calls me Sam. That is, everybody who's still talkin' to me, 'cause of my bad habit, see, bombing left and right—used to be just left, now it's all over the place. I need help!

Receptionist: Sam, I see what is crucial in any cure—you really WANT TO STOP!

Sam: Yeah, 'cause I don't have many friends left—except my pals the bomb makers. But they don't have to face all the countries I have to—they turn their backs on me!

Receptionist: (taking notes) That does happen to those with an addiction. But, do you have some relatives who are supportive?

Sam: I used to have a big family of nations, but only a few of 'em really like me now . . . they preTEND to, 'cause they're really afraid—

Receptionist: (writing) Afraid you'll . . . bomb them too? (with a little apprehension)

Sam: You got it! So (hits her desk top) you think you can help me? Do you?!

Receptionist: (leans back a bit) Of course. (stands) Dr. Anything has never given up on anyone's addiction, no matter how ghastly.

Sam: You don't seem afraid of me—

Receptionist: Of course not—(suddenly curious) Uh, you didn't happen to bring any little bombs with you today, did you? (nervous little laugh)

Sam: Nah, they're too big, I can't even carry them without help.

Receptionist: (light laugh of relief) Silly me! Dr. Anything will be right with you. (off)

Sam sits down in the chair, nervous, his fist hitting the desk top.

Sam: Boom! Boom! Here a boom, there a boom, everywhere a boom boom—Old Macdonald had a—Ho boy! (effort to pull himself together) Sit calm, Sam, calm, calm . . .

In comes the psychiatrist, Dr. Anything. He walks briskly, greets Sam, shakes his hand.

Dr. Anything: Glad to meet you, Sam. I'm Dr. Anything.

Sam: (stands) Hi . . . . what's your first name, Doc?

Dr. Anything sits in the upholstered chair on other side of the desk, picks up a pen.

Dr. Anything: Almost. Almost Anything. So, Sam, I hear you have a little addiction?

Sam: Big. Doc, big bombing! I need help!

Dr. Anything: And you will get it. Now, when do you think your problem began?

Sam: Well, I was always good with guns, even in my first war, the Revolution.

Dr. Anything: (writing in his notebook) That would be in 1776?

Sam: Right. We didn't have fancy bombs then, just cannons. I was darned good at them in all kinds of little skirmishes—France, Mexico, Spain, the Philippines, Nicaragua, but the real stuff came with World War II.

Dr. Anything: That would be in the 1940's, I believe?

Sam: Yeah. The Allies were havin' tough times, so I went there and hit those Nazi cities till they were a pile of rubble . . . then Japan—the big one, the Atom Bomb!

Dr. Anything: Uh huh. And how did you feel when doing that historic bombing?

Sam: (shakes his head) I felt pride! I was ending our war, saving lives of our soldiers—that's what I told myself! Only, I refuse to look at photographs of those cities after my bombing . . . don't ask me to!

Dr. Anything: Of course not. Now, what episode came next?

Sam: Next came the Korean War, just five years after the end of WW II . . .

Dr. Anything: And just how did that country provoke you to bombing?

Sam: Well, that damn North Korea was tryin' to push communism onto South Korea, see, and Harry couldn't let that happen, so I went right to bombing. Democratic little Harry Truman! God, we did have fun! (chuckles)

Dr. Anything Let's continue to the next episode.

Sam: A biggie . . . the Vietnam War . . .

Dr. Anything: Vietnam had attacked you, or some of your possessions?

Sam: Uh uh, this time little North Vietnam was gonna turn South Vietnam communist. The Cold War, we could do anything . . .

Dr. Anything: And now did you feel about that?

Sam: Not much of anything. But then, our men kept dying and the protests got bigger and bigger—Lyndon knew we couldn't win, but he wouldn't stop either . . .

Dr. Anything: And how did you feel then?

Sam: I forget. Then Nixon took over and let it drag on too.—I was getting darned tired of tossing those bombs and Agent Orange and all that—for almost ten years!

Dr. Anything: But you stuck to it?

Sam: Yeah . . . but later on when McNamara, Defense Secretary, said I killed 3,200,000 Vietnamese . . . I felt as rotten as he did!

Dr. Anything: Good, some self-awareness. Now, what came next?

Sam: Next, a poor little country, Nicaragua that had a lousy dictator, Somoza, whom the natives ousted. Our new president Reagan didn't like the new government.

Dr. Anything: Communists again?

Sam: Reagan kept calling them Commies and sent me there, so I dropped the heavy ones on bridges, water plants, clinics, buses—with no opposition!

Dr. Anything: And was this episode affecting your psyche?

Sam: A little, yeah, cause when the war was finally over, we paid the REAL Communist Party to join our coalition! What a farce, eh?

Dr. Anything: It seems that this episode had a negative effect on you . . . go on, please.

Sam: Yeah . . . (with some regret) 36,000 dead, and no real commies . . .

Dr. Anything: And the next incident of trauma?

Sam: A silly little country Reagan decided to attack—Grenada. (chuckles) A cockamamie little fairytale about rescuing some medical students. I shoulda kept out of it, Doc, but—no will power, see?

Dr. Anything: (in nice psychiatrist tone) It's very healthy that you can face the truth about your addiction. Now, what came next?

Sam: The Panama Invasion . . . George Bush the First. Late 1980's now . . .

Dr. Anything: How did Panama offend you?

Sam: Suddenly its leader wasn't doing our bidding. So we made up a story blaming him for all the drugs comin' into our country, and I dashed down there and did my thing—dexterously destroying six square blocks of homes, didn't miss a one!

Dr. Anything: And tell me, how did you feel this time?

Sam: (rises and wanders about) Heck, I was just bombing another little country that hadn't done anything to me, like it's my purpose in life! It gets in the blood! Ya gotta help me, Doc! (groan-sob, flops back into the chair)

Dr. Anything: I've had many cases of disgusting addictions. Continue in as much grisly detail as you can.

Sam: Okay, next came the first Gulf War—called Desert Storm.

Dr. Anything: Very pretty, sounds like a romantic movie.

Sam: See, Iraq pushed its troops into Kuwait to grab some disputed oil wells. Funny thing is—he had mentioned doing this to a woman from my country named April, and she said, "Well, we wouldn't really mind!" Ha! Famous last words! (chuckles)

Dr. Anything: (confused) But you actually DID mind?

Sam: (leaning forward) Yeah, other countries too, we all wanted that oil. I did most of the bombing, but England tried to keep up with me.

Dr. Anything: And how did you feel with this competition?

Sam: Nothing—I'm the best in the business! No scruples! So when Bush the elder told me to bomb their water systems, I happily obliged! (excited in recall, stands) It was such fun to see that water splashing all over, then the purification plant, the sewage plant! Blast here, blast there!

Dr. Anything: (a little anxious) All right, Sam, uh, let's move on to the next trauma.

Sam: (sits) After 9/11. Wow! Some crazy nuts doing what I'm so good at in other countries—but right in our city—New York!

Dr Anything: And who was responsible for that attack?

Sam: We figured it was Osama bin Laden, an unfriendly guy in Afghanistan . . . so we went after him. We couldn't tell which cave he was hiding in, so I bombed and bombed till I was ready to drop—and still didn't find him!

Dr. Anything: But was the bombing still satisfying for you?

Sam: (leans forward) This is when it began . . . to pale . . .

Dr. Anything: Why do you think that change occurred?

Sam: Maybe it was the day I was going to bomb someplace, it looked like a hospital . . . my generals were telling me to let the bombs go, "It's not a hospital," they said . . . but through the window I saw two little boys burned on their chest and stomach from my bombing that morning . . . burned so deep their nerves were destroyed and they couldn't feel the pain . . . their mothers there beside them trying not to cry . . . I waited by the window . . . by morning the two little boys were dead.

Dr. Anything (from now on showing personal reactions) And that was . . . a shock to you?

Sam: The first shock . . . I spent the next couple of days inside that hospital . . . lots of shocks to come . . . old women, young men, babies even . . . dead from my bombs . . . beautiful faces, alive at first, then by the end of the day . . . corpses . . .

Dr. Anything: So then . . . you didn't bomb anymore?

Sam: Not there, no.

Dr. Anything: And did you find this Osama fellow in his cave?

Sam: No. The new Bush gang was more interested in attacking a different country, Iraq.

Dr. Anything: Again?

Sam: Yep.

Dr. Anything: But now your addiction was much weakened?

Sam: (pauses) I wish you hadn't asked me that . . . I didn't think I'd ever bomb again, (rises) but the Bush gang, the whole Project for a New American Century guys—they'd been wanting this war for years! And when I saw it coming, I just had to get in there and show off my great talent again—Bombing! (moaning) The whole country has fallen apart—everybody shooting at everybody else—and me the best of them all! I couldn't even keep record of how many I killed, Doc! I'm ashamed of myself! You gotta help me, Doc!

Sam flops into his chair, head forward, weeping.

Dr. Anything: (stressed now) Yes, of course, I'll try, I'll really try. Now, why don't you sit down and have a drink of water. (pours water from a pitcher, one for himself also) And we'll take a little break, all right?

Sam: Whatever you say, you're the doctor. I'll just go visit the men's room.

He goes off. Receptionist returns.

Receptionist: Hi—my, you look exhausted, Doctor!

Dr. Anything: (leans on his hand, exhausted) Oy vey! That man Sam has a severe addiction! But I must do something . . . he's dangerous to himself . . . and to the world! But at least he truly wants to be cured.

Receptionist: Well, that's encouraging, isn't it? (sits behind the desk)

Dr. Anything: A little, perhaps—but CAN he change?

Receptionist: You can do it—that's why we all call you Dr. Anything. You can do miracles!

Dr. Anything: A miracle . . . yes. And I may have to change my name to . . . NOT QUITE Anything!! It will take a miracle at least to cure Sam . . . perhaps even the interception of—GOD HIMSELF!

FINAL SCENE FROM
"A NEW WAR, ANYONE?"

Some figures are sitting on the floor, watching TV news: The figures are shadowed and unclear; they will be revealed as dead soldiers from our previous wars.

News anchor: Questions still arise—Where are the weapons of mass destruction that the President told us existed in Iraq and posed a serious risk to us? Now questions are rising about Iraq's 's seeking uranium from Africa for nuclear arms.

The uprising in Fallujah has cost more than 50 of our fighting men, and our strong response has killed about 600 Iraqis—so far. Reports suggest that their heavy losses are inspiring other more neutral Iraqis to join forces opposing our occupation. Meanwhile, Secretary Rumsfeld has informed our forces who expected to be leaving for home that they will have to extend their tours due to the crisis and a shortage of military, and that troops will have to stay in Iraq for two to five more years to provide security—but will these added troops simply provide more targets for rebellious Iraqis?

In Baghdad, protests to the offices of Paul Bremer have complained that they still lack electricity and water for cooking and drinking. Reports of a few cases of cholera in south Iraq due to the impure water have prompted members of Doctors Without Borders to press for quick attention.

Columns in the New York Times by Nicholas Kristof and Paul Krugman and the Sunday morning talk shows all asked this morning—Were our intelligence agencies manipulating the truth about suspicion of WMD and Saddam's connection to El Qaeda? No doubt there will be quick and tough inquiries into the whole question of causes provided for this war, which has killed between 20 and 30 thousand Iraqis of all ages, as well as 600 of our own soldiers in military action, accidents and illnesses, plus many still-unnumbered suicides. More on this in tonight's news at 10.

He goes off. TV turns dark

The figures on the floor sit up taller, some stand, walk about slowly; they are the soldiers from former American wars. Gradually they all stand.

First soldier: Hardly surprising . . . remember the Tonkin Resolution? For that I died . . .

Second soldier: And how about rescuing our medical students in Grenada?

Third soldier: Too silly to be believed . . . but it was. I never saw them . . . but I lost my life anyway, on that stormy shore.

Fourth soldier: And of course we had to prevent communism from being passed onto South Korea from the North, so we intervened in Korea's Civil War . . . a long way for me to go to kill and get killed . . . .

Fifth Soldier: We didn't have to go far to stop communism in Nicaragua . . . President Reagan just kept reviling that "Dirty little Commie dictator in designer jeans . . ." Actually, he was Sandinista, and the Sandinistas had lost 40,000 people in their revolution to get rid of the terrible dictator Somoza, our buddy . . . . I wonder why . . .

Sixth soldier: A war little mentioned in the U.S. media, a sort of secret war . . .

Fifth soldier: True, only one American casualty, me (chuckling), Ben the silly clown,* mostly Nicaraguans dead . . . and when peace came, the U.S. arranged the election with a coalition of 11 political parties, including the real Communist Party . . . (quick laugh)

Third soldier: Why would they do that ?

Fifth soldier: The only way to beat the Sandinista Party . . . so we paid the real Communist Party for joining our coalition . . . clever . . .

---

*   Ben Linder, American engineer and clown, shot by a Contra as he was citing a spot for source of water

Sixth soldier: Immoral. Hard to remember just what the first George Bush gave as reason for his invasion of Panama, where he had been such a close buddy of President Noriega . . . something about drug trafficking by Noriega, suddenly so terrible that we had to storm in and kill peasants, destroy six square blocks of homes in Panama City to kidnap him and bring him here—hard to believe!—for trial and imprisonment . . . . I helped bomb those little buildings . . . before friendly fire . . . caught me . . .

Fifth soldier: What would they do if some foreign power came in to kidnap President Bush or President Clinton and killed as many Americans?

All the other soldiers: Declare War! War!

Seventh soldier: Yes, we can always find reasons for war . . . One of the more credible reasons for going into Afghanistan, because the government there had been protecting the terrorist Osama bin Laden . . . but they never found him . . . and killed thousands of Afghan children, men and women . . . and someone shot me . . . I never saw who it was . . .

Second soldier: I wonder if that country is in better shape now?

Seventh soldier: A brutal regime is gone . . . but no, the country suffered heavy bombing, and now poverty is as strong as before, and the warlords have returned . . . sad . . .

All the soldiers: Sad, sad, sad . . . all wars are sad, sad, sad . . .

First soldier: Hard to believe we are still starting wars, over and over . . . horror and death, horror and death . . . terrorism . . .

Other soldiers: Yes, terrorism, terrorism . . .

Second soldier: And the citizens, they still accept them . . .

Seventh soldier: So it seems . . . fly the flags . . .

Sixth soldier: Cheer the President . . .

Fifth soldier: Support the troops . . .

Other soldiers: The troops, yes, support the troops, before, like us, they die . . .

Another soldier comes up to them.

Eighth soldier: Yes, before they die . . . and after they die . . . for good reason and . . . for lies! For lies! (Angry but weak, bent over in pain and weakness)

The others come to him, offer arms to lean on, one on each side, others behind him. Ad lib words of comfort . . . we know, we know . . . easy does it, try to relax, let us help you, it takes time to accept death . . . but . . . rest now, we will go with you, etc.

They begin to walk off; the new soldier breaks away, distraught.

Eighth soldier: Never to see my little boy again! Never! (Weeping)

First soldier: Never to see another sunset . . .

All are walking off slowly now.

Second soldier: Never to travel to Italy . . . never . . . anywhere . . .

Third soldier: Never to throw a baseball . . . never to catch a ball . . .

Fourth soldier: Never to kiss my wife again . . . never make love . . .

Sixth soldier: Never see the flaming leaves of autumn . . . never paint them again, never . . .

Seventh soldier: Never hear beautiful music, Rachmaninoff, Chopin, Puccini . . . .

All are moaning "never, never, never as they slowly walk off through the audience.